Great Horned Owl Looking Over Snow Pile
(Kathleen O'Rourke, acrylic)

Snow all over, wind whipping 'round
Everywhere thick: white, green, brown
And still, it's coming down.

KATHLEEN O'ROURKE

WHAT I'VE SEEN
Animal, Nature, and Ranger Tales

BOOKSMYTH PRESS
SHELBURNE FALLS, MA

ISBN 978-0-9969719-2-8

Book and cover design by Maureen Moore, Ginger
Cat's Booksmyth Press
www.booksmythpress.com

This book is dedicated to Susie and Ellen
who held my hand every step.

Contents

Illustrations not otherwise identified in the text are

Introduction

S tanding alone on a high red-rock ledge, across from a band of bighorn sheep, in the backcountry of Arches National Park, all around me, as far as I can see, is what is often called wilderness. There are no humans for miles to hear me and I yell, "Look at where I am!"

I suppose I'm speaking to naysayers in my past, but mostly I'm thinking of my ancestors who traveled far to come to America, and I think of my younger self, a working-class kid, part of a large Irish clan from New York and Long Island, who never traveled, but wondered about the larger world out there. So, how did I get here, to live and work in this magnificent place out west? It's a winding tale, too long to tell it all, as all of our life stories are, but it comes down to "way leads on to way...."

It began one day after years of working many jobs, being a 42-year-old single mom with grown sons, and saying to myself, "Now where was I when I was 19? What were my dreams?" The question gnawed at me, and soon the answer unfolded clearly and easily. There is a certain magic that leads us along when we ask the right question.

The Outdoor Leadership Progam (OLP), a one-year certificate course at Greenfield Community College, in western Massachusetts, was what began my change of direction, opening up a world of possibilities. As an older student, I fit in fine. I'd always been physically active and enamored of the natural world. Of all her 48 grandchildren, Grandma referred to me as her "outdoor girl," and I still have the mittens and hat she knitted to keep me warm on my adventures around the neighborhood.

OLP taught me skills and gave me the support and encouragement to find work in the outdoors. I led canoe trips, taught cross-country skiing and assisted with rock climbing and backpacking programs, all the while getting more immersed in my love of nature and expanding my knowledge of wild foods and medicinal plants. Because I spent most of my time around outdoorsy people, I soon learned about the possibility of working as a naturalist ranger in the National Parks. It was perfect: I'd get to see the wild places in this country, not as a tourist which I couldn't afford anyway, but by actually living and working in incredible places I'd only seen pictures of. And the best part? My job was to learn all about the environment I was in, and then share that knowledge and love of the area with visitors.

It was not easy to get the job; I had only two years of nursing school and the one year of OLP. No college degree or veteran status, and few credentials to show for all my self-taught learning. But all the kids in my family (including cousins I grew up with) were brought up to work hard for what we wanted: keep your eye on the goal and you'll get there, eventually.

What follows are stories and snapshots of what happened to me as I followed my heart, spending lots of time in nature while I worked seven seasons at National Parks in the west, traveled and adventured between park seasons, and spent four summers living in a tent among tall red spruces while working as a naturalist on Mount Greylock, the tallest mountain in Massachusetts.

1

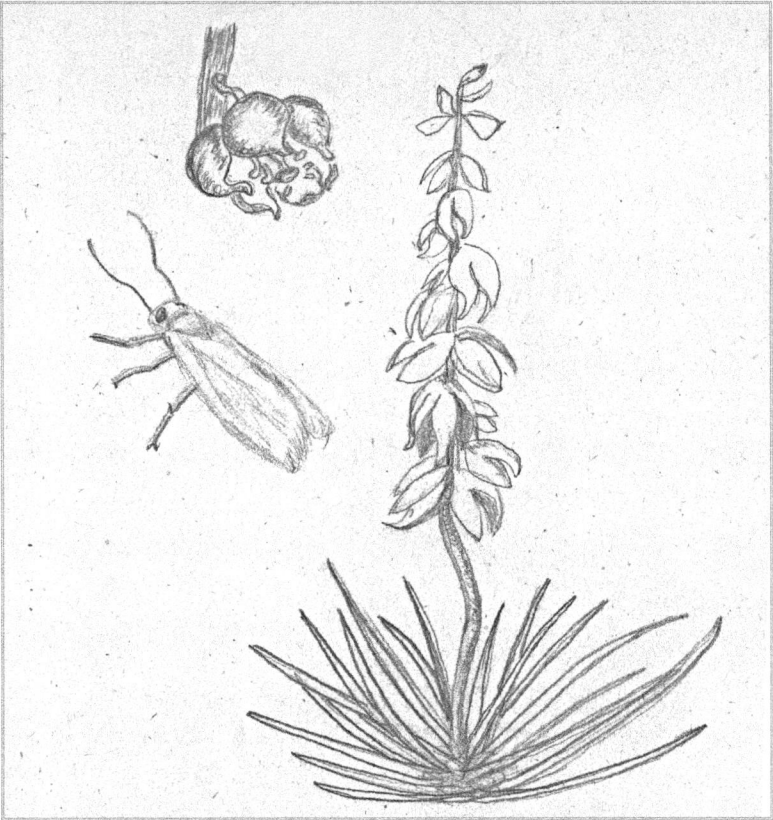

Time Goes Slowly

Natalie Goldberg, in her book *Wild Mind*, talks about laziness being necessary for a writer. Lying around, not doing much of anything, maybe not even getting dressed or brushing teeth one day, watching the sky, the living room ceiling, doing nothing at all. It's necessary; writing comes after that.

I think about the winter at Chaco Canyon, how alone I was before and after work, and on days off. I didn't have much in common with most of the park staff, and the people that I would have hiked and hung out with didn't live at ranger housing within the park. It was a lonely, mostly solitary time, and gradually I began to relax into this slowness and enjoy it.

My newly discovered fondness for being lazy fed my creativity. Navajo friends taught me how to clean and prepare the quills from a dead porcupine I had found, and I learned how to make quill necklaces and earrings. They taught me beadwork, brought me to the Trading Post where they got their supplies, showed me where to gather cedar beads from under the juniper trees, and laughed and encouraged me to keep trying for weeks until finally I produced a few quality pieces, about the skill level of a ten-year-old Indian girl.

AT unA vidA

I became fascinated with all the petroglyphs (pecked) and pictographs (painted) on the large boulders and canyon walls. I sat for hours in front of the pictures and drew what I saw. I marveled at the patience of the ancient ones who took time to peck hundreds of small marks to make each part of what appeared to be a long story of hunts, travels and births, and symbols and cycles of nature. If a picture was painted on the rock, I wondered what plants, or minerals were used to make such long-lasting rock art.

Birthing Petroglyph

Long hours were spent hiking and wandering about, watching how birds fly, following tracks, discovering hidden ruins, artifacts and rock art. Often I felt outside of time and there were a few mystical experiences when there seemed to be a presence of the Old Ones nearby, in the land. Those times would be hard to put into words later, but they were deeply absorbed into my understanding of life.

I had lots of time to read, listen to music tapes that Navajo friends gave me or friends back home had made for me of their favorite tunes. I drew and painted, wrote long letters, and I had time to just lay around, or to sit and watch out over the mesa, observing how Frajada Butte changed colors slowly at sunset, sometimes subtly, sometimes dramatically.

And I watched the sky. So often I just watched the sky and listened to the wind, the birds, and the silence.

After months of living this slow rhythm, I felt rising up in me the urge to write, and the same is true even many years later. When I allow myself time to be lazy—to simply be—stories and poems bubble up. Slowing down and taking notice can be so beneficial for us humans.

Grizzly

An Indian friend gave me a bear claw ring and told me that bear is the sign of the healer. I had cleaned his infected cut and given him some of my healing salve.

He talked about the respect that his tribe had for this animal. When I asked if people were afraid of the grizzly when they journeyed out alone, he said, "Not like most white people would be. That is because we understand that it would be an honor to have our life taken by a bear, just as it is an honor to take the life of bear."

This made sense to me. I've always wondered why we sensationalize animal attacks on humans and judge that as horrifying, yet humans who attack animals are praised for their sporting skill. I suppose the answer to this question has to do with the way our culture has, for such a long time, disconnected itself from the natural world.

Namaste

What is the proper salutation between people as they pass each other in this flood of life, each clinging to his piece of debris?
— *Leonard Cohen*

When I say, "Hey, how are ya?" sometimes it's mindless, but most of the time it is a verbal delight at seeing someone who makes me feel glad just because they're on this planet and I feel lucky to be sharing this time and space. Sometimes though, I can really feel that greeting to be "Namaste, I honor the light in you."

It's those times when I forget about me, or the other, and just recognize a divine spirit. Not the personality, or their looks, or the color of their jacket, but just their spark. Their light shining and my light shining. I think it might be like that all the time in the plant and animal world, but we humans have trouble believing in that greater capacity.

When I pick herb, I sometimes hear myself say out loud, "Oh, you're so beautiful!" And I know I have seen the plant's light, and the butterflies are noticing it, too. Bugs also like to be greeted and appreciated, worm or beetle or spider. They, too, are sharing the planet at this time.

When a momma bear stands up so tall on her hind legs, growls and greets me with aggression, I tell her not to be afraid, I won't hurt her babies. I back up slowly and leave, telling her that I understand because I'm afraid too. There's a part of me that knows we are of the same spirit. I'm sure of this. "Namaste" dear bear.

I wish I could do that with humans that are threatening and aggressive (and sometimes I have), but usually my spirit hides behind a wall of protection and we do not meet. Those are the times when we have both descended into the mundane world where spirits do not thrive.

I can meditate, yes, but it is the earth, the plants and trees, the birds and animals, the sky and the rocks that easily bring me home to spirit. So of course, that is where I go to learn about life, and to be peaceful with myself and with the world.

Dear Knee

Dear Knee,

I am doing my part and I wish you would do yours.

Okay, I'm begging. I need you; don't leave me now. You are important to me. I value your presence in my life. I'm thankful for all the great years we've had together: the sweet memories and fun adventures. Maybe I didn't always appreciate you as much as I should have. You quietly came to life when I needed you and perhaps I took you for granted.

I promise to care for you as you grow old. I will help you, protect you, listen to your needs and I will not make demands that you cannot fulfill. I will be there for you.

We will do T'ai Chi instead of jogging. We will use supports to help you move. We'll hike with ski poles to lighten your load, and we'll use great care on slippery logs and stones. We will no longer run down the mountain, hopping from rock to rock. That will happen only in our dream world where we are young and strong and fearless; where we don't know the future because we don't even think about it.

And we will dream deep and often, dear knee.

With gratitude,
Your supporting body

Protection

It's time to take off my winter coat.

In her book, *Solar Storms*, Linda Hogan writes about Dora Rouge's coat. It is heavy, matted, and very very warm—the skin of a bear. Dora Rouge wears it always, to stop the cold wet winter winds, and to cover her damp hot skin in July. It is her blankie, her "ga-ge," and even though she is a grown woman with a grown daughter, she needs her ga-ge. She doesn't think she'd be safe without her bear, and sometimes this has been absolutely true. The people understand and they do not expect to see Dora Rouge dressed like any other. They know she needs to feel safe, and then she can be strong.

I don't need my winter coat all the time anymore. Sometimes everything runs smoothly without it. I know this, but I've gotten so used to having this layer of protection, and giving up your ga-ge is hard, even when you are definitely a grown-up person.

I try pulling one arm out and peek around to see if I'm still safe. No one else seems to notice, so I take both arms out and tie my soft coat around my waist. I'm not really wearing it, you see, just kind of keeping it close by in case I need to hide quick or pretend I've got it all covered. Then I can relax and enjoy watching how you wear your ga-ge, if you are holding on tight with your pinky and think no one notices. They don't, you know, because we're all keeping safe at the same time.

Memo to Executive V.P.

Memo to Executive Vice President of Macintosh computers, and the person in charge of Employee Development and Workplace Enrichment:

That spider crawling up the leg of your desk does not want to be stopped. Not by you, or a cricket, or an air conditioner.

See that thin thread attached to your chair? That's its dragline, and no, it's not proof that you have been sitting there without moving throughout the entire morning. It took mistress spider only a few minutes to ooze out the arachnid silk.

So go ahead and push your chair back, break the thread, go get a cup of coffee, and by the time you sit down and roll your chair back in, there'll be another guideline. This time attached to your MAC plug wire. You don't unplug that until spring vacation, right? Let the fun begin!

Every morning now you will be given the opportunity for your brain to wake up gently, stretch its cells, imagine possibilities, and with ease you will begin to work and create brilliantly. Not from Java, but because your eyes are focused. Your new desk mate has grabbed your attention as surely as she has captured that flailing fly in its orb web. Grace has entered your sitting-at the-desk-world and you do not want this to end. A naturalist program may be all that is needed to complete this bonding.

We offer programs daily about the lives of insects and

other natural wonders of our world. When the spider eats that fly, you may not know whether to cheer or groan. But we guarantee that you'll skip your coffee break to watch.

Golden Eye

I am so far from civilization that even a helicopter
would not find me, but the owl in the branch
over my head hoots once, softly, telling me
I am seen.
The ravine that will be my path
is dry in August, but steep and littered
with obstacles in the way: large boulders
and small rolling rocks.
Placing each hand and foot carefully, crawling
slowly up, with eyes to the ground, suddenly
a loud "Wraaak!" and I fall over backward.
The bird is huge.
Above me, just where my hand had reached up
for the next large rock is a Golden Eagle,
startled from her perch.
Our eyes meet in an instant that stills time.
We are so close I see only a circle of yellow
staring down at me.
When the bird spreads her massive soft-brown
wings over me, I am in shadow.
The eagle rises up slowly and I think the fearsome talons
could pick me up and we would fly off together.
I am scared and awestruck and full of grace.
That one golden yellow eye will come back to haunt me
in dreams, on lonely walks—a comfort, a companionship.

2

Signing

I was on duty at a park in the badlands of North Dakota one morning when I noticed an older couple at the far end of the visitor center, signing to each other.

People were milling about, looking at displays and maps while gathering information about the park. They talked to me and to each other, sharing their experiences and asking questions about trails, animals in the park, and telling about their travels around this country. But the older couple was noticeably isolated, physically and verbally, from all the other visitors, so I went over to them, put my hand on the woman's shoulder to get her attention, then signed, "Are you deaf? Do you read lips? I know a little sign language."

The man and the woman became so animated, smiling, touching my arms and signing like crazy! I laughed and explained as best I could that I only knew a little sign. "Like a child would know," I told them, and, " I'm pretty bad

INTRODUCING A PROGRAM
WITH SIGN LANGUAGE

at finger spelling."

Through a combination of sign, pantomime and writing on paper, I learned that they had been to six national parks and no one had spoken to them. Six parks! Now they had so many questions about the parks they had been to, where they should go in this park, and how to best plan their visits to several more. They went to their car and returned with brochures from the parks they had already visited, road maps for planning their travels, and pictures of their families.

That did it. I cleared my schedule for the rest of the morning and thoroughly enjoyed getting to know these people and helping them plan the rest of their three-week trip. They were so happy and grateful, and I was amazed that my small amount of American Sign Language (ASL) was enough for us to have so much communication.

After that, I was resolved to introduce all my programs with sign language so that if any deaf folks were present we could connect; they would not be invisible. I also taught all of the visitors a few signs and encouraged them to speak to deaf people, even to just say "Hi." And then, in every park I worked at, any deaf people were shown my way, or to another ranger who signed. Eventually, I was given a name badge that said, with pictures, "I Sign," so people could easily find me. It didn't matter that I wasn't very good at signing; I just did the best I could, and besides, I've always been comfortable around deaf people.

When I was very young, my best friend was deaf. She lived next door, her dad, like mine, was a fireman, and our families spent a lot of time together. I don't remember any signs we did, we probably had our own way of communicating, like kids do, but I know it was during that time in childhood that I became so comfortable with what is needed to help a deaf person negotiate a hearing world: Being able to read someone's facial expression and body language; touching, tapping on the shoulder, pointing, gesturing. Lots of physical communication in general. And mostly, for those of us who can hear, trying to walk in their shoes and learn what might be helpful or what could be stressful when someone lacks one of our very important senses.

At another park when a deaf woman showed up alone for a strenuous hike, I asked her to stay with me, or right behind me when we had to go single file. Because I knew there would be some hikers who would want to be very near the ranger so that they wouldn't miss anything and could ask questions easily, I said to the group, "Alison is deaf; she'll be hiking next to me the entire time."

As we were approaching a bit of a narrow ledge, she tapped me, and I held out my hand. She took it and we walked that part together, then she released my hand and signed a quick "thank you." I doubt that any of the other hikers were noticing very much of the communication that went on between Alison and me during the two-hour hike. There were many quick touches, short signs and facial expressions, pointing and pantomiming; we were in constant contact but it was so subtle and easy that it wasn't obvious.

At a different park, the rangers give a cave tour for large groups, up to 30 people. Since I always began by speaking to the crowd in sign language, I quickly met anyone who was deaf, and also anyone with vision problems, claustrophobia or any number of fears or disabilities might surface at that time. It was good. I liked having the group know who we would all watch out for on the 90-minute tour through a dimly lit, and sometimes narrow, cave. If there was someone with us who was deaf I would not turn off the lights in the one large room of the cave. It's always a highlight of the tour for people to experience complete darkness, that truly pitch-black where your eyes will not adjust because there is no light at all. But it is simply too stressful for someone without hearing.

The higher-ups in the park didn't always agree with my veering from the standard and "making your own rules," but one of the naturalists, who was a disabled Vet, convinced them that he and I should bring some of our opinions and ideas to a disability committee. So Bob and I began advising and educating in "chain-of-command" style to the rest of the park. Bob would have my back and smooth out the edges when I didn't quite follow protocol. He'd scold me, laugh, and tell me I'd never be able to make it in the military. I told him of course I could, there's plenty of military in my family, I just don't want to. We became good pals that summer; he called me his hippie peacenik friend, I called him my big softy, bull-headed friend. We couldn't hike together, but we helped each other at work, enjoyed our similar brand of humor, and sometimes got together after work to write stories and poetry.

In the badlands, a Lakota man informed me that the Indians had used "Sign Talk" way before ASL was in standard use. Because the hundreds of tribes all spoke different languages, they had relied upon signing to trade, and to come together in hunts and councils.

I thought about doing a program for visitors to the park, and began to do some research, but I needed to know a lot more. Once I started asking around, it didn't take long for some locals with knowledge to surface. I was given a book or two to read, and Indian friends helped me to understand the many differences in the two forms of sign language. Their people did not use finger spelling, of course, and most of the signing was short phrases, easily learned and passed along. There were signs for greetings, counting, moons, winters, and many animals, which I taught the audience in the new program I called, "Indian Sign Talk." People got very involved practicing with their hands and kids had fun making up signs, and it provided an opportunity to talk about the different cultures, and how meanings can vary. Even though some signs were similar, there were many variations.

I had a favorite sign to explain this difference. In ASL, the sign for knowledge is pointing to the head, but in Indian Sign, you point to your head, then your heart and then bring your hands together. "Your heart must be involved with learning in order for true knowledge to be gained," a Mandan friend explained. The Indian signs were often graceful and simple, saying a lot with few gestures.

The program always ended with a favorite quote: *Signing can be used at a distance that the eye can reach, but not the ear.*

EVIDENCE OF A RECENT FLASH FLOOD, HORSESHOE CANYON, UT

Badlands Thunderstorm

I started running when the wind came strong and steady in a horizontal path. Leaning into it felt like a bucket of water was being thrown at my body, aimed precisely and with force. Here in the badlands, changes can occur with the speed of lightning. If you hear that loud thunderclap, you know you haven't been hit. Don't even worry about the next strike. If it does hit you, it will be swift and silent, the thunder marking the place of what has already been done. Lightning is the number-one killer of rangers in the backcountry.

I was scared, but I knew I couldn't go any faster. It might be only minutes before a flash flood separated me from my car on the other side of the wash. Once the water begins to trickle down the dry, sandy depression, it is foolhardy to think you can make it across. What might follow is a wall of water racing like a fast train and gathering into itself anything in its path. During my years of working for the national parks I had heard stories and had a few minor experiences, and so I learned to respect the destructive power of flash floods. Images of branches and brush decorating an old cottonwood tree ten feet up from the ground came to mind. My heart pounded from the combination of physical effort and primal terror.

There is something quite wonderful that can happen to us humans at times like this. A sort of peaceful resignation exists along with the fear: this is beyond my control, this is life at its majestic core, and nature is in charge. I began to experience my surroundings and the wild weather with a giddy sense of joy. The thunder felt like it was in my belly. The flashes of light made the world stop and glow, suspending time for an instant. The heavy raindrops obscured my vision and created a stream from head, arms, and legs, down into my boots. I drank the water spilling over my nose and blinked puddles from my eyelids. The storm was all around me and inside of me. If I could just see through the wind and rain well enough to place each flooded boot in the right direction, I would make it across the wash before it flooded.

I did not travel alone. To my right a herd of buffalo was passing by, 30 or 40 bulls, cows and calves, traveling at a pace a bit faster than mine, heads down, moving together like a great brown river. Wild turkeys screamed, squawked, flew, and ran in a messy frenzy. I was fully alive, senses were opened, animal-like, and I was alert and ready.

Four whitetail deer came bounding from the trees. One doe separated from the other deer and ran directly toward me. A quick attempt on my part to avoid collision failed and her shoulder slammed hard into my arm. Wet face to wet face, we exchanged startled glances before she ran off with the others. In that brief eye contact there was the realization that we are all equal out here: creatures of nature running from a violent storm.

I reached the car just in time. Water was coming fast and muddy down the wash behind me as I drove across. That night at ranger housing, warm in my bed after a hot bath, I saw the doe's eyes again. Rubbing the bruise she had made on my upper arm, I wished my wild sister good bedding and dry comfort this stormy night.

Snake Lessons

I reach into the cage, lay my hand on the bottom, and a five-foot constrictor snake begins to lightly wrap its body up and around my forearm. With snake's help, I begin my ranger program for the visitors and tell them all that I've learned about snakes in general, and this one in particular.

I've become quite fond and protective of this snake, and it shows. People can see how gentle I am with the reptile, and they see how snake responds by moving slowly and with ease over my arms and shoulders. This probably imparts more learning and changing of attitudes than any factual knowledge I can give them. But it wasn't always like this; before I began ranger work at the parks, I was terrified of snakes. It's definitely not cool for rangers to be afraid of the wildlife in their home parks. Visitors don't appreciate it, and they are very disappointed because you don't fit their ideal of the brave and all-knowing person who is at-one with the natural environment and can protect them if need be. So when I arrived at Theodore Roosevelt National Park (a.k.a. Northern Badlands) in North Dakota and saw a snake in a cage at the visitor center I decided it was time to not only get over my fear, but to become at ease enough to take snake out of the cage for impromptu educational programs for our visitors. It became a goal that summer season at the park.

But first, I had to have a burning question answered. Why do we, who are charged with protection of "natural resources" (and I don't like this phrase . . . nature does not merely exist as a source for human use), have any animal living in a cage? That felt all wrong. So I asked Jim, the head law-enforcement ranger. He was one person who didn't seem to think I was weird because of all my bumper stickers, which, in this generally conservative park, often brought a reaction like, "Well, I guess we know where you stand!" No matter what his politics were, Jim and I had a comfortable connection soon after my arrival as a newbie ranger at this park and I figured I could at least talk with him about my strong feelings of disapproval. Jim also worked as an EMT and a smokejumper who was frequently called out to fires at western parks. Since I'm a nurse, had also gone through EMT and First Responder training, and my Dad had been a NYC firefighter, we had an ease with each other, an understanding that didn't need to be put into words.

Jim smiled knowingly at my dismay, like he'd been asked

this before (probably by a naturalist ranger), and said, "Come on, let's get in the truck and go up into the park. I'll show you the reason." Several times he pulled over, we got out, and he pointed to skid marks that went off to the side of the road. Each time that we looked at tire tracks ending in the brush beside the road, we found a dead snake. Every time!

He explained, "Unfortunately, too many people think the only good snake is a dead snake. So, we capture a bull snake in June to help us educate visitors and maybe save a lot of snake lives over the summer. Then we release it back to the wild before cold weather sets in. A bull snake is usually pretty docile, but it looks a little like our prairie rattlers and it even mimics them by vibrating its tail in dry brush to sound like a rattle. That's a great tactic for discouraging its predators, all except the human ones who think the snake is dangerous, and so they try to kill it. Think of our caged snake as a volunteer ranger. It gets some pretty good treatment and appreciation from the staff."

Now I became even more determined to make our snake's confinement worth its loss of freedom. It took a while.

Two of the young rangers, lovers of all animals, dedicated themselves to helping me reach my goal because they thought it would be so much fun. Rangers don't have the usual entertainment and social life that they've had back home, and this would certainly make for some entertaining evenings. We waited until the Visitor Center closed for the day and, with a plan, we entered the back door after dark by punching in the code that would disable the alarm system. This was probably illegal, but we really didn't know that at the time, and besides, we had such honorable intentions. Once inside, with only the dim lights that were kept on all night for security reasons (snake robbers?), Tom and Tonia took the snake from the cage and began to slowly introduce us—my body to snake's body. They stood on either side of me, holding snake's head and tail loosely, while I felt its skin and how it moved, and then I held the middle. At any point I could step back and say, "That's enough for now." My teachers were patient and gentle, with me, and with snake.

This continued for a week until, finally, I was able to hold all of snake by myself as long as my friends were nearby. It became so satisfying to let snake have some time to move freely outside the confinement of a cage that one night we sat on the floor and just let snake go wherever it wanted to. It only took a few minutes until that snake got a taste of freedom and moved faster than we had ever seen, right through the open door leading to the small theater where many visitors came each day to see a short movie about the park. We searched under all the seats, up on the stage, over by the exit door, but snake was gone! Now we were really in trouble! You wouldn't have guessed that, though, by all our laughing.

We began imagining all sorts of scenarios: snake moving up someone's leg, entering a backpack or purse left on the floor, moving across the stage under the lighted screen like it was part of the show, or some kid squealing with delight, "Snake, I see a real snake!" and visitors screaming and running from the darkened room. It was all too funny; snake escaping to freedom. But after another hour of searching everywhere, we finally gave up and went back to ranger housing, no longer in jovial moods. This was serious. We'd be in big trouble once it was discovered what we had done.

Naturalist rangers are beloved by park visitors, but they are the peons in a system that sometimes can have some pretty power-hungry people at the top.

So we were worried that night. But Tonia, who was more concerned for snake's well-being than what might happen to us, got up at dawn, went to the Visitor Center before it opened and found snake easily. It was coiled on the table that held its cage. She shrugged and matter-of-factly said, "Guess it missed its familiar home." For the rest of the summer, this young woman was my hero, so brave and compassionate.

I began to give regular programs for visitors, becoming more comfortable and fond of this snake. A turning point for me happened with a group of school children, as I was talking with them while holding snake loosely over my arms and around the back of my neck. All of a sudden, snake started to constrict and move fast, and then flicked its tongue in my ear. It had never done this before and it was alarming until the children alerted me to a young boy standing behind me who was harassing the snake by making fast hand movements at its head. I put snake back into the cage and used this as a teachable moment about how animals can be scared of people when they make abrupt movements or come too close. The fact that snake, when it became very stressed, neither bit me nor constricted as tightly as it could have, made me even more dedicated to giving programs and teaching people about snakes.

A typical spontaneous interaction with visitors might have been a child wanting to hold the snake along with me, or a scared but very curious adult who just wanted to watch me handle snake and to feel its skin. When I would tell the people that I had been very afraid of snakes when I first came to the park, they wouldn't believe me. But I explained that we all, especially adults, have a tendency to be afraid of what we don't know, what is unfamiliar to us. So, if someone said they hated snakes, I'd respond, "Oh, you're afraid of snakes?" This became very funny one day when a man kept insisting he "hated the damn things, and there are no good snakes, and besides they're ugly as hell," and on and on.

Each time I patiently responded with, "Oh, you are afraid of them." He eventually became pretty annoyed with me, "You sound like a broken record!" Meanwhile, his wife and several visitors who had gathered around were enjoying themselves immensely. It ended with him saying, "I got nothin' against you, ranger, but you're dead wrong. If I ain't afraid of grizzlies, I sure ain't afraid of a little bitty snake!" His wife touched his arm and said, "I know how brave you are, dear, but I think you are just a bit afraid of snakes." The people around them smiled gently and nodded in agreement.

As they were leaving, he held back, came closer to where I was standing, still holding snake, and said to me, in a low voice, "Okay, I'll consider what you said. Maybe like you did, I just need to get more acquainted with the darn things."

"That's a great idea," I said, "I thank you, and snake thanks you." He left with a big grin on his face, and I bet it wasn't because he was thinking of killing the next snake he came across.

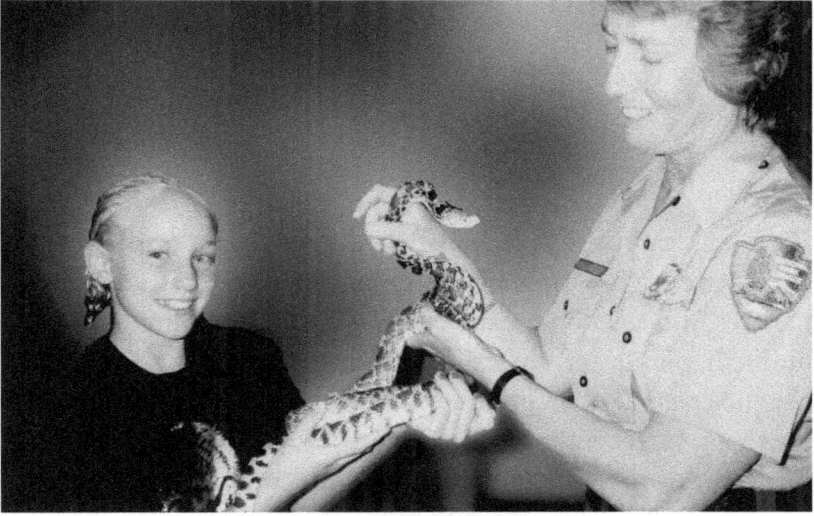

A YOUNG PARK VISITOR GETS COMFORTABLE WITH SNAKE

Wind

In some cultures, it is said that the wind is a reminder of how we are breathed by life-giving air, and how our breath exhales into the one breath shared by all of us: animals, birds and fish, plants and trees. The soil and rivers also contain air that has passed through other life forms. We may be inhaling air that was recently exhaled by a fox, a chickadee, a neighbor's cat, or the large maple down the road. If interconnectedness of all beings is a difficult concept to grasp, we have only to be aware of the air we all share. The wind will remind us when we forget.

In North Dakota the wind blows steady across hundreds of miles and only an occasional tree, butte or ravine will impede its full strength. It was here I spent a ranger season

at a national park, and in my programs for the visitors I told about the turbulent history of this land and its people. This made the park officials nervous and they said I could not continue with such extreme teachings. Luckily, a few of the local Indians with whom the park wanted to maintain good relations, also became aware of the controversy and said to me, "If it is true, tell it." And so I did, all summer.

For a very long time, in the mid-1800s, the Indians had resisted an order to leave their land and live on a reservation. General Phillip Sheridan had gone before Congress to convince its members that one way to get the Indians to comply would be "to starve the people onto the reservations." When hunters, shooting for sport from the back of trains, drove the buffalo from the plains, it brought about the result the government had hoped for. The end of the buffalo herds meant that the Indians could no longer follow their traditional ways of life. Now the Indians who had been reluctant to leave their hunting grounds, would finally be forced onto the reservations. Starvation will do that to a people. Submission, so that the children will sleep again at night, the pain in their bellies soothed by food. And so they went to where the food was.

In the winter, when the wind blew with ice on its breath, the people were cold without their warm buffalo robes. The cavalry solved this problem by leaving smallpox-infected blankets outside the earthlodges. The children and the elders, the most thin-skinned, were suffering in the chill air and so they wrapped the wool around their bodies and put their noses close to the scratchy warmth, and breathed in. They died first. Then the others. And soon there were not enough people still alive to exist as separate tribes.

"That is the story of how our tribes came together," Gerard said. We had become friends during my first week at the park. Plant people recognize each other easily, across a room, across time and cultures. It was during this time that we found that we shared many other common ways of being. Even the history of our ancestors had similarities.

"Because so many of our people died, we could not go on as we had before," Gerard explained. "That is how I came to be Mandan and Hidatsa, and my cousin, Keith, who you will visit at Knife River next week and help set up a teepee, is Arikara. These three tribes came together so that we can continue as a people. Not enough remained of any one tribe, and so we have joined since then in order to survive.

"We live with the wind," he told me, "it is the great breath that breathes us as it does the animals we hunt. When the buffalo dies, its last breath is given to the hunter so that life may continue. When the grizzly bear killed an Indian, his last breath was given to the animal. That is why we believe we are all the same. The wind and the breath of our ancestors live in all of us. The animals and plants have always known this."

Coyotes

REPLACING FENCE POSTS KNOCKED DOWN BY BUFFALO. RIDING WITH BACK-COUNTRY RANGERS ON MY DAY OFF.

There's not a lot to do in badland country after putting in a long physical workday. So rangers frequently entertain themselves by watching the ever-playful and interesting communities of prairie dogs that coexist with the bison as they make wallows in the dirt, creating quite a ruckus. On special nights, the northern lights become visible, waves of violets and yellows and blues, but mostly greens in long streaks of bright green in the dark sky. Out here, there is no light pollution to block or dull the spectacular show.

The youngest rangers often came to life in the evening, and their frisky urges led them to a butte where they would do their best imitations of coyote yips, barks and howls. Eventually this was responded to by the pros – a pack of coyotes calling back, giving away their location with the same abandonment as the humans. One night, after this communal howling, a ranger said, "Whenever I feel lonely, I come out here and it helps. In this lonely place, knowing the coyotes are there helps."

So, one lonely morning I started a hike in back country just after dawn, wondering if our nighttime wild friends would show themselves in daylight. I've always had a fear of dogs that I don't know, but somehow the thought of coming upon coyotes caused me no uneasiness.

After about a mile, a coyote appeared in front of me, down the trail a ways, easy to spot in this open country. He crossed from right to left, looking at me all the while as he climbed a butte. I was pleased, but then coyote came back, circled in a wide loop around me, and again climbed the butte, watching me from there.

Curious behavior, I thought. He seemed to want to keep me in sight as he continued going back and forth, and circling in closer around me. If he was trying to get my attention, he had! I was puzzled, but decided to just continue hiking, thinking he might follow. Then I heard the barking of a different coyote close by, off to my right. That coyote was staying where it was, but continued to make threatening noises and postures at me, similar to what dogs will do when being territorial.

Now I was beginning to feel some fear, but I was still puzzled, until I heard the high-pitched yips of pups. That's when I spotted a den behind the fierce mother coyote, and I could make out the movement of at least two furry balls behind her. I had to laugh at my slowness in recognizing what had been going on since I saw the first coyote. I explained to her that I was a bumbling human who hadn't taken the obvious warning from the male coyote when he'd tried his best to lead me away from the den.

I turned back to the direction I had come from, saying to the mother, "I'll be going now, but perhaps we'll sing together later tonight."

Litter

This list was posted at many National Parks in the West:

How Long Will Litter Last?

	Years
Cigarette butts	1–5
Aluminum cans and tabs	500
Glass bottles	1,000
Plastic bags	10–20
Plastic coated paper	5
Plastic film containers	20–30
Nylon fabric	30–40
Leather	up to 50
Wool sox	1–5
Orange and banana peels	up to 2
Tin cans	50
Plastic 6-pack holders	100
Plastic bottles and Styrofoam	indefinitely

Echinacea Journey

I was often privy to information about medical rescues in the parks, probably because I worked as a nurse between many of the park seasons. That's how I met Gerard, head ranger at a remote unit of this northern badlands park and one of the very few Indians to work for the National Park Service in the 1990s.

Gerard told me about a visitor who had been bitten by a rattlesnake in the back country. The man, who was an athlete and a jogger, saw the snake stretched out across the trail in front of him and in half a breath's time, he made the wrong decision. He began running and leaped up and over the snake. In the time it took for his first foot to leave the ground, the rattler coiled and struck his landing foot. Gerard found him a half hour later and knew it was a bad bite. The man's foot and ankle were purple, swollen and mottled. He loaded the man into his truck and raced to the hospital, two hours away. The jogger was in great physical condition and that's what saved him. That's also what made him think he could out-run a snake.

Gerard told me, "In the old days we would have used Echinacea instead of going to the hospital." That made me curious about using the wild Echinacea that grew out there. In the western grasslands, the wild *Echinacea angustifolia* is smaller and more scraggly (and more potent) than the purpurea species most of us are familiar with. But none of the books I researched, or the people I asked, could tell me exactly how it was used for a snake bite. I wanted specifics. When a Lakota Sioux medicine man that Gerard arranged for me to meet also did not have the information I was seeking, my Mandan Indian friend said it was time to ask the plant.

He spoke about how in the past the Indians learned by watching the animals. They also experimented to discover which plants were useful and they passed that information along to following generations. "And sometimes," he added, with a bit of a smile, " they made mistakes and people became sick or died from poisonous plants." He believed that the tribes long ago were so connected to their world that they were able to know things that we don't. He suggested that I try to sense the knowledge I was seeking by hiking alone, far into the back country.

I went on my next day off. To avoid the intense heat of the day and the sunburn I was sure to get (as one Indian friend said, while pointing to my reddish skin, "And they call *us* redskins!"), I decided to set out before dawn. For hours, my only companions were bison, snakes, pronghorn antelope, birds and coyotes. By 9 a.m., the sun was already hot, my steps had slowed, and my thinking mind had come to rest. I had experienced this feeling many times before, when I blend in so completely that I'm just living through my senses.

At one point, I came up out of a shallow ravine with my head down, absorbed in the discovery of a plant with a tight white tuft on its top. My hand reached out, felt the tuft, and squeezed it between my fingers. The result jolted my sleepy mind awake. The little tuft had separated and grown to a mass of soft fluff. In my hand was a ball of cotton; surely the people long ago found many uses for this plant. As I lifted my head to see the trail, I fell over backward, startled by a loud grunt and the foul breath of a huge buffalo bull who had been standing at the top of the ravine. I usually speak to animals in situations like this, so I apologized for surprising him and said I'd go back down the ravine and come up a little ways away to give him space. "You are a lot bigger than me,"

I added.

All morning a young coyote had been stalking me, playing, or just exhibiting its natural curiosity. I had spotted it at the beginning of the trail, when it was busy shaking a

snake that dangled from its mouth, soon after dawn. Like a cat with its mouse captive, it dropped its prey, pounced on it, leapt back and took it up in its mouth again. I watched until the coyote spotted me and quickly ran over a butte, the snake hanging limp in its jaw. For the next several hours, coyote appeared and disappeared many times. As soon as it saw me watching, it ran off. I wondered how long it was watching me each time before I sensed its presence and turned to look. It was a good game and I enjoyed this companionship on my long hike.

As I passed between two large buttes, the land opened wide before me and I saw acres of *Echinacea angustifolia*. I made my way toward the center and sat down, squinting my eyes to fully absorb the purple haziness all around me in this isolated place. For a long time, all was still and the only sound was my own breath. Then my fingers dug, and I began chewing the small root. The taste was strong and biting. My lips and tongue grew a little numb and tingly. I spit the gooey wad into my hand and put it on a swollen insect bite on my calf. Then I tied my bandana around my leg to hold the poultice in place. My brain kicked in, this made sense! I immediately knew that's exactly how The People used the plant for snakebite. Internally, the Echinacea helps to fight any bacterial or viral infection and boosts the immune system; externally, it would be absorbed somewhat locally and help to reduce swelling, pain and nerve damage.

"Oh, I know, I know!" I yelled out. Coyote appeared from behind the butte (probably startled by the sudden intrusion on the silence of this place) and I held up the stem and flower of the plant and yelled, "Look, Coyote, I found a knowing!"

The following week when I saw Gerard, I related my experience to him and he laughed. "I do not think any book could have told you more," he said.

Now I understand that's the way it works. When you open to a plant, it tells you its secrets and there are many ways the information comes to you. The plant helps guide you along your learning path.

3

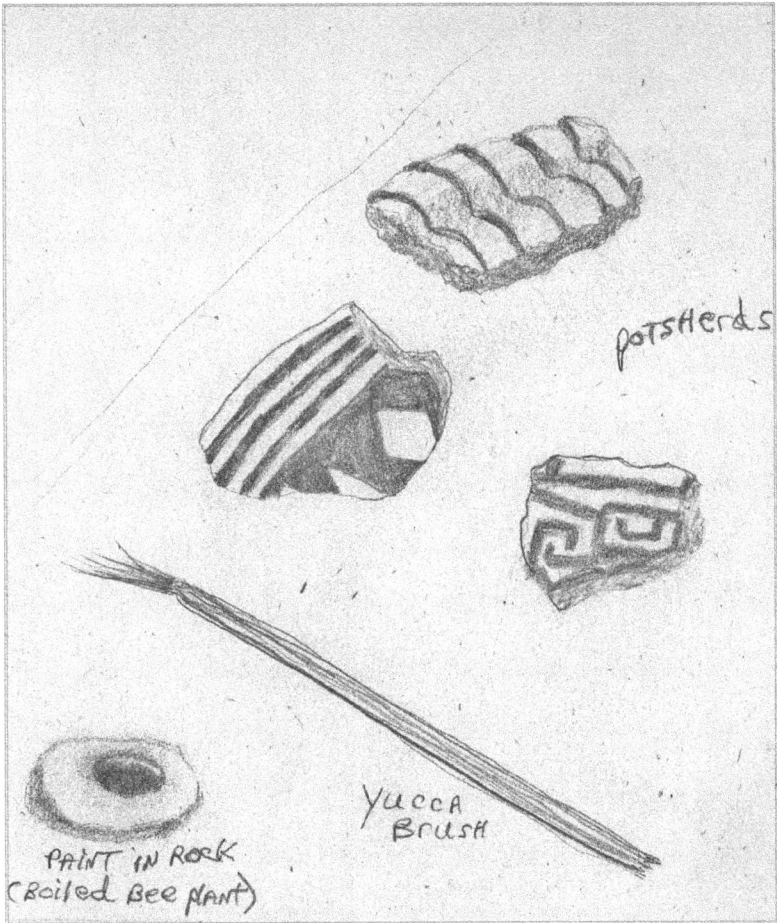

potsherds

YUCCA
BRUSH

PAINT IN ROCK
(Boiled Bee Plant)

Mountain Lion

I am afraid of the big cat: its secretness, its intelligence, and especially its potential for swift violence. I know if it attacks, there will be no warning. Like a lightning strike, the damage is done before you hear the thunder.

On this remote backcountry trail of Arches National Park, there won't be another human being, perhaps not even for several days to come. I could choose to turn back, soon find my truck, and then drive the rough, washboardy road back to a well-used trail. But I am here today, and so is a mountain lion.

I continue on, placing more distance between civilization and myself. This is just what I want to experience, and want to know deeply. The vastness, the heat, the quiet, and the aloneness. I am aware that this is real life; this is the world, as I want it to be. Not complete, but whole. I accept my fear and understand my place here, knowing how small and unique that place is in the circle of life.

I pay attention to my breath and glance across the wash to the low sandstone cliffs on my right. She is there and she sees me. All of her senses are more fully developed than mine. There is nothing to do, so I just keep walking and stop at intervals to admire her large tracks where they had crossed the trail, disappeared on a long rock, then reappeared further along in the bottom of a dry and sandy wash. Today we share our world, and I am grateful for the honor.

The cat is probably doing what is often referred to as a "curiosity stalk," and it is my curiosity about the cat that keeps me moving forward through the fear. I can feel her presence, even when I don't see her. There have been a few other times I have felt what I've also heard others describe as, "the hair raising on the back of my neck." Once, in the backcountry of Canyonlands, I felt that sensation and looked across to see a mountain lion on a ledge, far enough away that I wasn't afraid and could appreciate how his tawny fur blended in beautifully with the color of the rock.

Another time on a very remote small trail in Nevada, below a purplish alpine meadow filled with thousands of shooting star flowers and blue birds nesting and flying about, I entered a narrow section of the trail, boxed in by huge rock walls. I was singing and merrily making my way down when an intense feeling overtook me. Maybe it was the claustrophobia that can sometimes bother me, though I usually ignore it, but this time the fear was bigger than that. When I returned and told a friend who lived below the mountain range, she smiled knowingly. "Yeah, I know what you mean, that fear that comes up and you feel it on the back of your neck. It was a cat for sure. Perfect place for one too."

When finally I reach my destination, a hidden arch, I sit under it, to cool off in the shade and enjoy my lunch before heading back along the trail I came on. I hadn't spotted the lion in quite a while, but when I begin my return hike, all along the trail where my footprints were are new prints of the cat. It intrigued me, was she behind me on the trail when I no longer saw her along the nearby sandstone cliffs? Or did she descend and walk the trail while I was eating lunch and enjoying the view? The cat's footpads were everywhere, alongside or right on top of my recently made boot prints. It's obvious, this is her territory, not mine.

My fear is gone now. Tired and mellowed by the peace and quiet, I walk along, interested in how our steps are so close or together. I know this was a rare and special day that will stay in my memory. Today, cat is with me and I will be with cat.

Archaeology

There's a small town in southern Utah where a poet lives. The other residents of this town were not familiar with poetry and most didn't read books much, either. They were, however, familiar with archaeology because many small ancient Indian ruins had been unearthed and studied by archaeologists visiting their town over the years.

The poet, a retired professor, had written many wonderful poems during his lifetime and he had a desire to share them with others, and also to continue his role as an educator. So, in secret, he began to put his poems out there. Some he buried in flower and vegetable gardens. One was left under loaves of bread at the bakery, another by the leg of a park bench. He left poems under rocks and piles of leaves, tucked inside a school dictionary, taped to the underside of the playground slide, and behind the stop sign at the corner.

A young boy was the first to find a poem. It was tied to a branch of a juniper tree. Then a woman dug one up from her garden along with the carrots. A young mother discovered a poem under the seat of her child's stroller and a very old man found one taped inside the lid of a metal garbage can when he made his monthly trip to the dump.

Soon the entire town was searching for poems and exchanging what they had found with each other. Some put their found treasures in boxes where they kept collections of bones, rocks and feathers. Others began writing their own poems and burying and hiding them all over town. In a few years this tiny town was known as a place where many poets and archaeologists lived.

The poet professor was pleased. He was growing old in a town of kindred souls.

Hiking in Arches

DELICATE ARCH

I'm taking a rest in the shade of a pinyon pine tree, on a comfortable juniper log that's shaped like a bench, and there are big fins of Entrada sandstone rising up all around me. It's my last week at Arches and I have all day to rove trails, so early this morning I had driven up the 18 miles of park road, passing Balanced Rock, the Windows, the road that leads to Delicate Arch trail where I hiked yesterday, and finally to the end of the road where I began this day-long hike, in backcountry, on the Primitive Trail.

I've only seen two quiet hikers so far; otherwise, it's just been me, the birds, the mule deer, jackrabbits and, perhaps, a mountain lion who would see me but stay hidden from my view. As I hike across the more open desert parts of this trail, I look for coyote. The tracks are here, and scat too, but like cougar, he is an elusive animal.

It's been warm enough this past week for lizards to be scurrying about. They make me smile, these little dinosaur-looking critters. Sometimes there'll be one warming itself on my doorstep at ranger housing when I go out in the early morning. ("Good morning lizard. What do you plan for this sunny day?") I'm hoping to see a snake or two along the trail, but it's probably still too cool for them to be out. The only sound besides an occasional gust of wind is one canyon wren welcoming spring back to Canyonlands with its song of high notes descending to low, like a spiral, beautiful and graceful.

After five miles, and hours of hiking a challenging trail, I've already eaten two or three times, drunk more than a quart of herbal iced tea I made last night, and now I'm at the farthest point of backcountry, at a tall rock formation called "Dark Angel." Here, I leave the trail to climb down rocks and look for ancient petroglyphs on the face of a sheer rock wall. I remember this spot from ten years ago. It's a Class-lll site; few people other than park rangers know where it is. When visitors ask where they can find Indian rock art, we will tell them about front-country sites, but not this one. It's protected by Dark Angel and park rangers.

High up on a sheer cliff, there's a large patch of whitewash, and with binoculars I can see the nest I expected to find, but it's too far away to see if any chicks are in it. The white is a good way to locate raptor nests. The birds poop just outside their nest and the white color stains large areas of the cliff wall. A perch from which the birds hunt would have less whitewash and it would be more scattered. I can see a large bird riding the wind currents in the distance; it looks like a Red-tailed Hawk by its flight, wing shape and color. They live out here, as well as Golden Eagles, Cooper's hawks and Great Horned owls.

In the distance is the trail I'll follow back to where it winds up a steep rocky knoll to Double O Arch. Off to my right, beyond the red-rock cliffs, spires, fins and the vast expanse of desert are the La Sal Mountains, all covered in snow. I'm surrounded by the blue, purple and white of mountains, the browns and reds of desert and rock, the green of pinyon pine and juniper trees, and a blue, blue sky with soft, slow clouds.

On the way back, two more miles to go, I stop again. I don't want this day to end, but the low sun is a reminder that soon I'll have to meander down, over and through rock fins, toward Landscape Arch, then hike the easy one mile out. I don't know that I'll ever be here again, so I let my eyes absorb everything around me, and my ears and nose fill with the sounds and smells. Here, it seems like the quiet extends for hundreds of miles. It's a paradise and I'm feeling grateful that I've had so many places to experience heaven on this blessed earth.

SACRED DATURA
DATURA meteloides
POTATO FAMILY

First Mountain Lion

Years before I learned that I could safely walk where cougars live, I had my first scary experience in Canyonlands of Utah. Hiking alone along a dry, sandy wash of backcountry, I came to an abrupt stop. I asked myself, "What made me stop just now? What is so strong that my eyes, ears and mind got interrupted in their activity? Was it a smell, or something just below my awareness? What is it that made me stop?"

My mood took on a hyper alertness; I scanned the horizon all around. Something felt threatening – I was very afraid. My skin prickled, breaths came faster and more shallow, the fine hairs on my arms and the back of my neck felt brushed up. I've been scared before so I know to pay attention to my breathing, try to slow it down, take a few deep breaths. That has never worked in situations like this, though. Instead, I did what has always been helpful: I talked to myself and to "out there."

"This is a beautiful, peaceful day, but there is something for me to be aware of. I am not here to harm, and I wish no harm to come to me." And I babbled on with random thoughts until I became calmer.

Finally I realized that I was close to the big rocks where a ranger clearly saw a mountain lion a few weeks before. Looking at the ground, I saw the imprint of the large round pads of the cat's feet. "Oh," I gasped, "It's you. And I'm here too. Are you watching me? You're so quiet in this hidden canyon."

I wondered if I should turn back. I told myself, "There haven't been any attacks by lions in this part of Utah that I'm aware of. It's perfectly safe to go on. The animal lives here and is, of course, curious about anything that enters its territory."

My reasoning was sound. I was 99% sure that I had nothing to worry about. But I turned back. Some days we are brave, and some days we easily become nervous and can't regain our balance once it's out of whack. I went back.

"Goodbye, and please don't follow me. I'm being a scaredy cat today."

Explosion

It was early in the morning when the explosion happened just beyond the large rock formation to the north of Arches Visitor Center. It shook the building and stopped all conversation. People grabbed onto a counter or reached for a wall or the nearest person to them.

We didn't know it then, but a major gas line had ruptured when one of the bulldozers miscalculated and hit it hard, causing gas to spew out fast into the surrounding air. A spark from a passing 10-wheeler ignited the huge vapor ball, trapping the trucker and pipeline workers in the black smoke and fire.

Those of us at the visitor center got out with only the shirts on our backs, and I spent the rest of the day at the medical staging area two miles south of the fire, along with a few other rangers, firefighters and grieving families (we all assumed no one could survive such a disaster), while the helicopter flew overhead. Everyone was banned from the explosion area and the road was closed until we knew what had happened and where the fire was heading. So, hours later, when the seven pipeline workers and one trucker emerged from the smoke, there was a deathly silence, punctuated only by a few gasps or startled sobs. They came so slowly, walking, hobbling, leaning on one another, all covered in black soot. It was impossible, what we were seeing: walking black clouds. Where were we? Was this the same day? Surely the world had disappeared and time had stopped.

In that pause of disbelief, 50 or so people, were all staring, eyes widened, no one speaking, afraid to believe what we

A SMALL PART OF THE BURNED AREA

were seeing. One of the blackened men fell, and that's when we all awakened from the dream and quickly stepped into our humanness. Everyone was alive...how could that be?

At a picnic table, I sat with the men who didn't require an immediate ambulance ride to the hospital. They spoke of the miracle of how the trucker jumped from the burning truck and how one of the guys knew the big rocks up there and led them out. They held on to each other, crawling from one safe area where they could breathe to another. They didn't know if they'd make it out, or if the fire would encircle them. The workers were as stunned as all of us at the medical staging area when they finally saw daylight that afternoon.

Pipeline Blast

A natural-gas pipeline exploded near Arches National Park on Thursday morning, injuring several construction workers and closing U.S. 191 from Moab to Interstate 70.

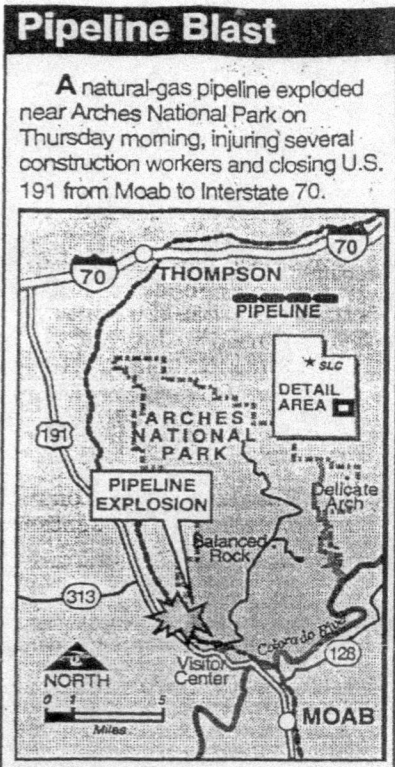

THOMPSON
PIPELINE
SLC
DETAIL AREA
ARCHES NATIONAL PARK
PIPELINE EXPLOSION
Delicate Arch
Balanced Rock
Colorado River
Visitor Center
NORTH
Miles
MOAB

Mike Miller, Todd Adams/The Salt Lake Tribune

Utah Highway Patrol Sgt. Darrel Mecham, who was supervising a roadblock on Highway 191, said that right after the blast, he and an Emery County Sheriff's sergeant hiked up near the cliffs to see if anyone was trapped.

Mecham said their were eight or nine vehicles incinerated by the fireball, including the bulldozer, but no victims were found.

"It blew several of [the vehicles] across the highway," Mecham said.

He said workers told him that they had only three minutes to run away from the escaping gas before it blew, and said it was "absolutely amazing" no one was more seriously hurt.

Initial reports had as many as eight people dead, 60 injured and a dozen trapped. It turned out that only four workers required treatment at Allen Memorial Hospital in Moab. Three of those suffered minor injuries. A fourth required surgery for an unspecified internal injury.

Although the injuries were not as severe or numerous as first feared, medical teams from neighboring Carbon, Emery and San Juan counties were prepared for the worst, as were doctors and nurses from Salt Lake City, Grand Junction, Colo., Farmington, N.M., and Page, Ariz.

60

Within a week, it was back to routines at the park: raise the flag every morning at the park entrance, take the weather specs from overnight and record any precipitation and the high and low temperatures in the daily log book, listen to morning report on the park radio (another rock fall in the Maise district, a mountain lion spotted in backcountry of Needles district, a search-and-rescue training in Canyonlands for any new staff), and then check the schedule to see who you'd be working with that day. During that week the head EMT/law enforcement ranger and I often talked with each other, still trying to process all that happened on the day of the explosion. He mentioned that we were very, very lucky. If the gas ball hadn't been set off by the truck, it would have taken about one minute to roll down Bloody Mary Wash and explode at the first spark it came to: the visitor center where we all were that morning. The knowledge that we came that close was added to the general trauma we were still sorting out and trying to integrate so that we could start feeling normal again.

On my day off, I needed a break from the anxiety that seemed to be with me so often during the day and night. I wanted to feel some healing, perspective, security, and familiarity, so I climbed the hill, up into the park where a band of bighorns often roam. They were there, with their stillness of peace, comfort and life. I sat on a rock and hung out with the sheep for a long time. They had also experienced the explosion that shook the earth, and seen the billows of black smoke rising from the fire. Now they stood so quiet, looking my way occasionally, not bothered by my presence. We were close, in a small side canyon, and time stopped for a while. Here, there was space enough to hold the disaster that had suspended life and created a before and after. With the bighorn, it was just now, and we were safe.

4

Ravens

Porcupine Lessons

Even in fading light with dark shadows
of twilight in these woods,
he is easy to identify by movement alone:
that sluggish, hesitating, wobbling
but steady, heavy stepping from side to side.
Knowing that rhythm of motion is helpful
by day, and with luck, by night.

Have no fear, this animal will not move
faster than you, and when the porcupine runs,
it's hard not to roll on the ground with laughter.
But please, can't you see
he is already a little embarrassed?

Step aside, let him pass,
maintain dignity for the both of you.
But watch closely, for he has lessons
to teach about pace and steadiness....
and staying the course when moving
under pressure from here to there.

Bye to Greylock

Every year on Mount Greylock, I ended the season with a personal ritual at dawn. A goodbye to the mountain and a gratitude for my three months of living in her embrace.

My tent was completely hidden in the red spruce forest —tall enough to stand in, and roomy enough to allow for a comfortable size foam mattress for my sleeping bag, a cooler/table, box of clothes and books, a small rug and a low beach chair. The extra tarp I rigged up over it also made a bit of an awning where muddy boots and dripping rain gear could be removed before I entered my home in the forest. Except for one tornado, one hurricane, and two extreme thunderstorms, the tent stayed mostly dry for the four summers that I lived on the mountain.

The nights of being flooded out, or when the tent poles collapsed at 2 a.m. in a violent storm, and even that early morning when so many trees were pushed over by the strong winds, were frightening at the time. But those were rare occurrences and somehow became as natural to life as every morning greeting the rose-breasted grosbeak that had a nest in the red-berried elder bush by my tent door for the entire summer. Or the raven, flying over from Ragged Mountain at the same time each morning, whom I relied upon to call me awake soon after dawn if I had overslept.

I loved being a part of this simple world where nothing was strange or weird, or demanded skills from me that I did not already possess. Back in town I am sometimes at a loss in negotiating my way in the world, especially when it comes to technology. But on the mountain, I was free and calm and capable. I learned that even after a week of drenching rain, I could be cold and damp day after day, and survive, even enjoy life as I bond with my fellow animal creatures who were also out in the weather, going about their lives.

So, when the end of summer came and leaving the mountain meant carefully packing everything with visions of it all being ready to easily unpack next June, I began that last day, every year, with the same ritual. Before any light was visible in the sky, I bicycled out to Sperry Point and sat on the massive rock ledge, waiting to greet the dawn. It came slowly at first, and I wanted to notice and remember every second that passed. How the old-growth forest across the deep ravine became visible. And how only one bird would sing tentatively, a solitary vireo, then the flute songs of hermit and wood thrushes, and finally, they were joined by the calls of several red-eyed vireos, all eventually blending into a practiced chorus.

The small river below caught a piece of light in one curve, and that began to travel the length of the flowing water spilling down from the Cataract Falls. When it was full dawn, I wrote a poem that the mountain gave to me as a parting gift.

Sunrise at Stony Ledge

First, a foggy haze, behind a darkly veil.
Then, slowly
>*in silence*
creeping
Mount Prospect rises - fog spilling down
her steepest flank - and meets the underbelly
ledges of Robinson's Point.
A pale outline of dark trunks and conifer shapes
touches the deep space of receiving valleys.

Hermit thrush feels the arriving light
and sings the new day here in this
amphitheater of air, space, soft peace.
It is always the first to wake when night
blends into day and I await the flute melody.
For a while only we are here: greeters of the dawn.

It is the same each summer, though the fog may shift,
clouds form and fade away, and colors surprise anew,
it is the same each summer.
No matter the changes that shake our worlds,
here, it is the same.

I wrap these minutes in memory and I will open
this gift on a cold winter morning;
see the colors,
hear the flute
feel the space.
This dawn will be greeted again and again.

There is comfort (joy, too) in knowing it will be here
when I am not.

Back at my tent, I often found a poem from Croo, the fun-loving young people who worked on staff at the summit lodge or on the trail crew:

Ode to the Naturalist

I feel bad for them
The skunk cabbage eaters
the dandelion feeders
the herb garden breeders
the petters of porcupines
the eaters of nettle spines.
They live in the trees
they give thanks for fleas.
In a world without walls,
they are easy to please.

Raven

It took only seconds for raven to lift off a twisted
locust branch, spread its tail and wing feathers,
and let its leaving be known with a throaty caw caw!
All the while the chickadees continued their short,
choppy flights to a tray that held sunflower seeds
just enough for a day.

Back and forth, back and forth, with a grace
to the way they took turns, flying, landing, eating,
in a beautifully balanced
piece of choreography.

Raven also was watching, from the top of a white pine tree.
Neither he nor I could take our eyes from this rhythmic dance
of tiny synchronized fliers.

Tenting in the Rain

The week in July when it rained for seven days and seven nights changed forever my understanding of what it feels like to be uncomfortably and consistently damp.

The large, old tent didn't leak but raindrops pooled around the edges and followed thin, long roots of the spruce saplings that reached under the bottom tarp, making the tent floor squishy even while it remained dry in the center.

Each day I moved the sleeping bag and pads, my clothes, gear and boots, the cooler that held food, and a box of field guides a few inches farther from the sides of the canvas. By the end of the week, I slept in a tight, crowded space that felt like a small, cramped closet. Claustrophobic, here in the vast mountain wilderness.

This was one of the few experiences of living in the woods that reminded me of our human needs and frailty. The rest of the time I blended in with the slow gait of the porcupine, the lumbering bear ahead on the trail, and the heavy branches of balsam fir that brushed my hat and splashed my face as I passed by. But all this rain, that was different!

I wished for the easy acceptance of my animal and bird neighbors, who did not yearn for a weather report, who lived each day just as it was given, holding no anxiety over tomorrow. So I watched and learned.

By the fourth or fifth day, it no longer mattered that I woke, once again, to rain. I began to appreciate the marvel of my completely waterproof skin. I no longer could smell my own dampness, or had any concern about the mildew growing on my boots. I gave up, gave in, and became more animal-like and comfortable in this growing kinship with the creatures and the wet earth. And there, I grew.

Tips for Tent Living:

- Have a comfy bed. A mattress from a Volkswagen bus worked nicely with flannel sheets, a sleeping bag when needed, and a good pillow.

- Use a gallon plastic tub with a lid for a pee bucket at night. Put an old towel under it (to catch any leaks), and then pour it around the periphery in the morning to mark your territory. Most animals respect this subtle communication.

- Have two good flashlights with extra batteries. Maybe one could be a headlight to enjoy reading in bed at night. A candle lantern is good for outside, but not in your tent.

- String an extra tarp over your entrance where you can take off wet and dirty clothes and boots. Hang your clothes to dry inside and put your boots on a small old rug just inside the door. A dry, clean tent feels cozy and warm.

- Keep a gallon jug of water for all sorts of cleaning up jobs, and a second one with potable water for drinking, washing and teeth brushing.

- Have several small towels that can be used to lay wet gear on, and for any mopping up or sweeping out the floor.

- Remember how lucky you are to have this experience. Fall asleep to forest sounds, raindrops, or complete silence; wake to the call of raven, hermit thrush, and solitary vireo.

Wet Bear

Hiking up to the summit, I take cover under a giant spruce
as rain spills over its gnarled roots and finds a course
downhill to my tent, dry and sturdy, sheltering my possessions.
"Let it rain," I shout, looking northeast
toward dark and layered clouds, smokey and moving fast.
The wind comes thick as a scratchy towel
then soon changes to a soft embrace.
This temporary tree shelter is made of boughs
that shift with the wind. The ground is deep and porous,
old red spruce decay. It smells of home.

It is summer. I do not feel the cold.
I have lived on this mountain, slept here, becoming more
related to my wild kin with each change of season.
I am an animal with waterproof skin.
This steep rocky path is familiar after four summers
climbing and descending, at dawn, in twilight, in storms.

It rains for a week.
I become a snail,
          a salamander,
                    a dripping leaf.

In the morning, climbing up the mountain is less lonely.
A bear is leading the way.
In the wet mud is only that paw print, mine is next.

Where bear slips and slides, I am careful.
Rounding a turn in the trail, I see the dripping
hairy backside of my companion. In this hard rain,
each of us lowers her head, steps slowly and methodically,
one foot in front of the other. Breathe, step, pause,
and keep on climbing this mountain.
We are sure of the way, bear and I.

5

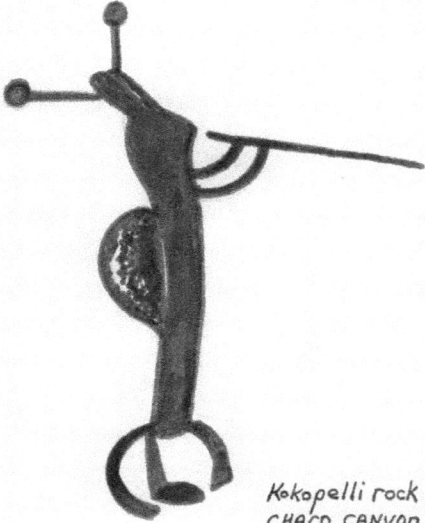

Kokopelli rock
CHACO CANYON
N.M.

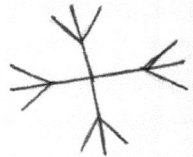

Kokopelli rock
CHACO Canyon
N.M.

wijiji site, CHACO, N.M.

Listening, and Learning, the Navajo Way

On a backpack trip in the fall, a friend and I drank a quart of water each day before setting out in order to lighten our packs. I learned this from the Navajos.

A long time ago when the *Dine'e* – The People, the Navajos— took off for a day to tend sheep or make a journey, they brought no water with them. This is in the desert. Before they left they drank large quantities and saturated their tissues so they did not become dehydrated or feel a terrible thirst.

My Navajo friend, Tucsohn, says he is an old man. I do not see him as old – we have different cultures, different ways of seeing. A Navajo Indian will often refer to someone over 50 as old. This is good; it means respect. Tucsohn was a singer for the Blessingway Ceremony until his voice became weak and his body could no longer stay awake during the long days and nights. A tribal singer must be strong, physically as well as spiritually. Tucsohn hikes (he says "walks") in the desert. He goes far, all day, and he may stay out for the night. He brings only a small pouch of pollen; that is always with him.

Tucsohn follows the old ways. Phoebe says he is a traditional. She is a modern young Navajo woman: gets a perm, paints her nails red, drives a Subaru. But she has not traveled far from the reservation or from her clan. She has made intricate beadwork of her own designs since she was very young. When it came time to learn rug weaving, her grandmother said she must learn to find the plants used to dye the sheep's wool. Phoebe balked at that. "I can buy the dyes," she said. "I don't know how to find the plants and they are too hard to learn." Grandmother insisted: If she wanted to learn from her, she must do it from the beginning.   Phoebe respects her grandmother; she is learning to weave the old way.

Tucsohn speaks in stories, often lapsing into his first language - Navajo. I could not always follow him, but I knew not to interrupt. This I learned early on in our friendship when I had asked a question, wanting him to clarify what he was saying. He stopped talking, looked at me, and then walked away. So I learned. For some reason I'll never understand, he decided to give me a second chance. A Navajo will never interrupt you, and when you are finished speaking, he or she will patiently wait just in case there is something you have forgotten or might want to add.

There were many more stories from Tucsohn, and I began to listen with my heart and my senses instead of just my head. Traditional stories are told after dark, in the winter before the first thunder and after the first frost. I heard stories from Tucsohn about animals and birds, how the weather and

ANASAZI RUINS AT CHACO

moon give us signs, who the Anasazi were and why they disappeared, and how The People came to this world.

When coyote was shot, it was Phoebe's sensitivity and Tucsohn's stories that helped this Anglo through a painful experience. I had seen coyote almost daily as I did my nine-mile ranger patrol around Chaco on my bicycle. I was

COYOTE IN SAGEBRUSH

often teased by the Navajo maintenance and office staff or the other rangers when I arrived back at the ranger station, soaked because I had been caught in an unexpected rain or snowstorm. I preferred my bike to a park truck because I could hear the ravens, smell the sagebrush, discover hidden petroglyphs on the canyon wall, and see my elusive friend, coyote.

The day I heard the shot I was hiking up on the mesa. The sound startled me, and as I looked down toward the road I saw a grey truck drive away. I climbed down through a crack in the canyon wall and was met by two visitors who told me some sort of animal had been shot. I knew—right then I knew. I rode my bike to where I had seen the truck and found coyote's tracks leading into the brush. When I got to him, he was lying on his side, eyes open, and blood coming from his side. I touched his fur, still warm, then sat next to him as he died. I took my time saying my goodbyes and did a ritual, a funeral for coyote.

My voice was shaky on the park radio when I reported the incident, and upon arriving back at the ranger station there were jokes and lots of questions and paperwork to be filled out by the park police. No one seemed to realize the grief I was feeling. Except Phoebe. She looked at me a long time, and then said, "I heard your voice on the radio; it did not sound like you." "I'm sad," I said. She nodded, "Yes, you are."

The following morning it was difficult to be inside working in the visitor center and so, when I saw Tucsohn shoveling snow off the walk, I went out to shovel with him. We worked in silence until he said, "It was a Navajo who shot coyote."

I was stunned. The park police didn't know who had done the shooting, and Tucsohn had not spoken to them. "How do you know? Why would a Navajo shoot coyote?" The questions came rushing out, but the answers were for my understanding, not for the police. This park was on land that once belonged to the Navajos, and this shooting was Navajo business.

"But why? Why? Coyote was so beautiful, he didn't hurt anyone!" Now I was close to tears. Tucsohn leaned on his shovel, looked at me and smiled, and began a story.

"Coyote came up in the emergence with the insects. He said he could cause trouble for The People. Then he said he would throw this stone on the water and if it stayed on the top, it would be all right; if it sank, The People would die. So

80

he threw the stone and it skipped across a few times, then it sank. That is why The People think it is bad luck when a coyote crosses your path. Harm may come to you. So you have to break coyote's spirit, kill him or sprinkle corn pollen on his tracks. Some people will reason with coyote and that can help. When coyote crosses your path he is talking to you, so you have to reason with him."

"Would you ever kill a coyote?" I asked, not sure I wanted the answer. He looked at me, reached in his pocket and pulled out a small leather pouch. "It is not necessary; I have my corn pollen." Then he told me the person who shot coyote was probably a young Navajo. "Many of our young people no longer follow the old ways – they have lost their shield." As he said this, he made a circling motion with his palm flat around his chest. I understood this to mean they had lost their spirit.

Tucsohn continued to tell me about coyote: "Coyote is a messenger to The People. A Navajo got bit—that has never happened before. But coyote was trying to warn The People about the asbestos plant that will be built on the reservation." I was beginning to understand that coyote had many meanings for Navajos.

After several more comic stories of trickster coyote I was laughing along with Tucsohn at how naive and sly coyote was. My friend stopped his talking, picked up his shovel, and said, "Tears and then laughter—that is good."

My heart got the healing it needed, and my head began to realize that there are many different ways to understand what happens in this world. And, I learned to listen.

Death

The old Hopi Indian said, "Life is a circle
and when we die, the circle is completed."

Navajo friends also told of this circle of life
ending in death: "We are all born with our own circle,
some very big, some very small.
It is different for each person,
only The Great Mystery knows our circle."

That winter, on the reservation:
A baby nine days old stopped breathing at night.
A drunken young Navajo drove off the road into a rock wall.
The old man who ran the trading post was shot in a robbery.

The Indians grieved quietly, spoke in low voices,
and nodded to one another without using words.
Woven within this was always the gentle humor
that accompanies all of life.

There was no speaking of:
- Not fair
- Too soon
- Such a shame
Or, Why, Why, Why?
No need for questions when the circle has been completed
At nine days, at 17 years old, at 65.

Bobcat Trails

The ranger housing at Chaco Canyon, with a large picture window that looked out to Fajada Butte and the surrounding mesa, was the best of all the parks I had worked at. My entire apartment at the previous park could have fit into the living room. In the winter, late afternoon when I left work to walk through sagebrush on the path leading to housing, I'd enter the dim rooms without turning on any lights and sit in a chair in front of the large window, just in time enjoy the setting sun in this open landscape and big sky.

FAJADA BUTTE FROM MY WINDOW

The first night I saw the bobcat, it was a complete surprise. As he walked past the window, he stopped and looked right at me; only a few feet and a pane of glass separated us. Certainly, I had never been this close to a bobcat, and at first I felt a little uneasy. Then I got curious and began to study the animal, its ears and eyes, its whiskers and paws, the fur, the face markings. He just sat there, very still, and continued to look right at me. When I moved a little and the cat did not respond, I realized he could not see me; I was sitting in the dark. But the window probably had become a great mirror when the setting sun reflected off the glass. The bobcat was looking at himself.

Almost every night for the next three weeks, the cat came by at about the same time and stopped for several minutes to look at the glass, at the mirror, at me. Then he'd just continue along on his way.

I began tracking the cat's wanderings during daylight (he had made quite a trail along the wall by staff housing), but eventually I'd lose any signs of him as I tried to follow the paw prints through dry sandy washes, and over and around rocks.

When the cat no longer came at twilight, I wondered where he had gone and decided to explore further when I had the time on my next day off. I found his tracks, then once again lost them, until I finally gave up and just continued meandering around, enjoying the scenery, the rocks, the ravens. When I climbed up a hill to get a better look at some petroglyphs on a rock wall, I came upon the tracks again and soon discovered clues about what might have happened to the bobcat.

I'd assumed that the animal had changed his evening routine and was now making different paths somewhere else, although I knew there could be any number of reasons why he no longer came by. There weren't any biologists at the park that winter that I could ask. But suddenly, here in front of me, was a story to unravel.

There were many tracks all over the place in one small area, as well as a little fur and spots of blood on the sand, and many large and small feathers from a raptor. "Owl," I thought, but really, that was only my best guess. What I did know, from the evidence, is that a large bird, hawk or owl, attacked the cat by using its talons and beak. But a bobcat is no rodent or rabbit; he fought back mightily and it looked as if he got away by running to the nearby rock face, which had plenty of cracks and spaces where he could hide from the bird.

The bobcat might have died from its injuries, or from an inability to hunt, and perhaps the young owls did not get any more meals from their injured parent. The web of life and death is so easy to see in this vast desert landscape. And, sometimes, we are woven into the story for a little while.

FAJADA BUTTE

In Beauty May I Walk

The old woman walks the mesa above the canyon, stopping miles before her hogan, unable to step farther. Her breath is coming in gasps now.

This has happened before; she knows to wait. The wind will come in the afternoon and breathe for her. She does not try to make happen what is clearly not able to happen. The woman knows she is not alone; the elements are all around her, and also the creatures. The sun and moon and earth accompany her on this journey.

The woman sits in the partial shade of a small juniper tree and waits patiently. There is nothing else to be done and she is sure of this. A calm heart allows her to be carried on the Beautyway Trail. It was good she learned this way as a young girl. Now, in her old age, there is not so much trying, there is more just being on the trail of beauty. She does not know where it will lead her; that is not her business. Only to keep walking, or at times carried by all that surrounds her, remembering to take rest. To stop, to smell, to listen and look, touch the warm comfort of the sand, and wait for the wind.

Ravens entertain, playing at chasing one another, calling out their raspy cries, flying straight up then quickly turning over and around: loop-de-loops. The old woman chuckles, remembering hours of enjoyment in her past, watching these birds by the canyon wall in Wijiji, when it was her people's land, before the park came.

She notices her ease now with breathing. In the west the wind stirs up a dust devil, the message wires of the spirits.

She waits; the air around her quickens. She opens her mouth and allows the wind to enter. Before the sun sets, she will be home. Led by the wind - her prayer and her path will take her there.

In beauty I walk.
With beauty before me may I walk.
With beauty behind me may I walk.
With beauty above me may I walk.
With beauty all around me may I walk.

> *Hozhoogo naashaa doo.*
> *Shitsiji' hozhoogo naashaa doo.*
> *Shikeedee' hozoogo naashaa doo*
> *Shideigi hozoogo naashaa doo*
> *T'aa altso shinaagoo hozoogo naashaa doo.*

In old age wandering on a trail of beauty,
living again, may I walk.
It is finished in beauty.
It is finished in beauty.

———————————— ◆ ————————————

This is from the Navajo *Night Way Prayer*. The word *beauty (hozho)* has a very different meaning in prayers like this. It was explained to me that the word means happiness, goodness and beauty, living in harmony and in balance. And so much more that cannot easily be translated into English.

Christmas on the Rez

On Christmas Eve a few of us friends went caroling on the Navajo Reservation that surrounds Chaco Canyon.

At the first place, we pulled up facing the house and blinked the truck headlights several times before turning off the lights and the motor. If the old man who lived alone out here in that run-down trailer wanted to hear us sing, he would open the front door slightly. We waited several minutes in the dark until a light went out inside the house. "No, not tonight," my friend Phoebe said, nonchalantly.

The houses are far apart on the rez, and the roads are not in good shape, so we only visited three houses in all. At the other two, where old couples lived, we sang, *"Laa–naa ya-a-t'eeh-go Kesh-mish . . .* ("A good Christmas to you, sung to the tune of "We wish you a Merry Christmas").

I had been regularly practicing this song, along with a few easy Navajo phrases I was learning, but my vocabulary was still pretty limited. So I was more like a back-up singer, joining in randomly with the words I knew. My pronunciation, however, was excellent, thanks to my teacher.

Phoebe had been gently drilling me almost daily as I went through the repertoire of words and phrases she helped me to learn. Her head close to mine, she'd peer into my mouth and say, "Where is your tongue?" She coached me on how to push air around and over my tongue to make the correct sound. My friend had decided, after I told her a few Gaelic words, that Navajo would not be such a difficult language for this *bilagaana* (white woman) to pronounce.

By the time we arrived at our last stop, her cousin's house, we were chilly and tired of driving around, so we settled in for a visit. I wasn't sure how many people actually lived in the small house; my guess was six or seven. A few people stood, or sat in chairs, or puttered around in the kitchen, which I could see from my place on the couch where I had been led to take a seat, alone. I was a little embarrassed, being treated like such a guest, but two little boys soon put me at ease.

"Kat-lin, would you like some juice?" the older child asked. I responded with sign language and told him that would be very good. The younger child asked, "Red or purple juice?" I chose purple.

The little one disappeared into the kitchen with his brother and they returned with a large red plastic cup filled with purple juice. As they stood in front of me waiting for me to taste it, I took a drink and realized it was grape Kool-Aid.

"Yum! *Ahe'hee* (thank you)," I said to the boys who now took seats on the couch, one on each side of me. They sat quiet, lightly kicking their dangling feet up and down, and smiled big every time I took a sip. "Very yummy," I said to them, as they giggled softly, never taking their eyes off me.

The adults in the house were mostly getting some food prepared in the kitchen or talking quietly in the room where the boys and I sat.

There was one silent presence in the corner. An old woman sat on a stool in front of the blanket weaving she had apparently been working on when we showed up. She was wearing traditional Navajo dress: a velvet shirt, a long skirt, deerskin moccasins, and turquoise and silver jewelry, belt, and squash-blossom necklace. She appeared to be very old and was simply called "Grandmother" by everyone in the house.

I greeted her in my best Navajo, and also signed, "*Ya'a'te'e'h ah ben-e*" (Hello, how are you). The boys liked that I spoke with my hands, but I don't think they knew sign language; the grandmother also approved of hand talk and was probably more familiar with this way of communicating from the old days. She said a few words that I didn't understand and I realized that, like many of the elders on the reservation, she did not speak much, if any, English.

I had become quite used to being around people who were all speaking in Navajo or Hopi, frequently punctuated by soft laughter, and I never felt ignored or uncomfortable. Actually, I found their voices rather soothing. Occasionally, someone would speak in English if there was something I should know, or to give me a brief idea of what they were talking about.

Sitting on the couch that evening with those two delightful, but quiet, children was very homey. I'd be going down to Albuquerque in a few days to visit my many cousins there, and I thought about how the cozy warmth I experienced in this Navajo home was similar to the feeling among my cousins.

I had some small candy canes in my pocket and handed one to each child. They looked toward Grandmother and she nodded to one boy and then to the other, and they took off the wrapping and began to suck on the candy. I got up and brought one to the old woman, she put it on her lap and then took my hand, turned it over, brought it up to her face and breathed on my skin. I remembered Phoebe once explaining to me that Indians are not big on hugging or shaking hands the way Anglos do. If they do shake hands, it is done very gently ("no pumping up and down!"), and the old people will sometimes greet family and close friends by taking their hand and breathing on the back of it. "They are giving you their breath, and that has special meaning." So I felt honored; it felt like a hug.

When I sat back down, Grandmother nodded to me, and the boys both looked at me, waiting. I realized I was also to enjoy a candy cane, so I took one from my pocket. Another nod, more smiles, and we three of different generations enjoyed our sweets together on Christmas Eve, just as it should be.

Kachina

The tall young man was outside carving wood. He stood at a roughly put together table that was high enough for him to work at without bending over. His wife and three little kids were nearby, out in front of their small wooden house on the mesa. I greeted him in Navajo, which also passed for a brief salutation in the Hopi language, and we fell into a leisurely afternoon conversation.

There had been a protest march the day before that I heard about on Indian radio; he said his uncle was one of the organizers. "They want to put a ski place on the mountain. It is sacred to our people, and even the Forest Service, who are often good neighbors, don't understand." We stood and looked at mountains far in the distance.

When Grandmother comes outside the little children become her helpers. They bring a chair for her to rest on, fetch a blanket from the house, and soon a drink of Kool-Aid and a peanut butter sandwich. And they stay a while, leaning into the old woman. Perhaps there'd be a story.

"This is life," the man said, pointing to the huddled bodies. "It is good, like this. For our family and the old ones, but especially for the children."

Then we talked about the young people. I wondered how they were doing, if there was much trouble with alcohol and drugs on the reservation. He told about how they have their own museum now so that they can sell to the tourists. "If they learn the old ways, they stay out of trouble better. So we teach them to carve these Kachinas. It is sacred work and it calms them. That's how I learned. Uncle brought me here to the Second Mesa. Now I carve and don't drink. Right, wife?" We three nod, and smile big.

The next time I looked, the two smallest children had fallen asleep, and the grandmother too. They were not hurried; there was nowhere to go.

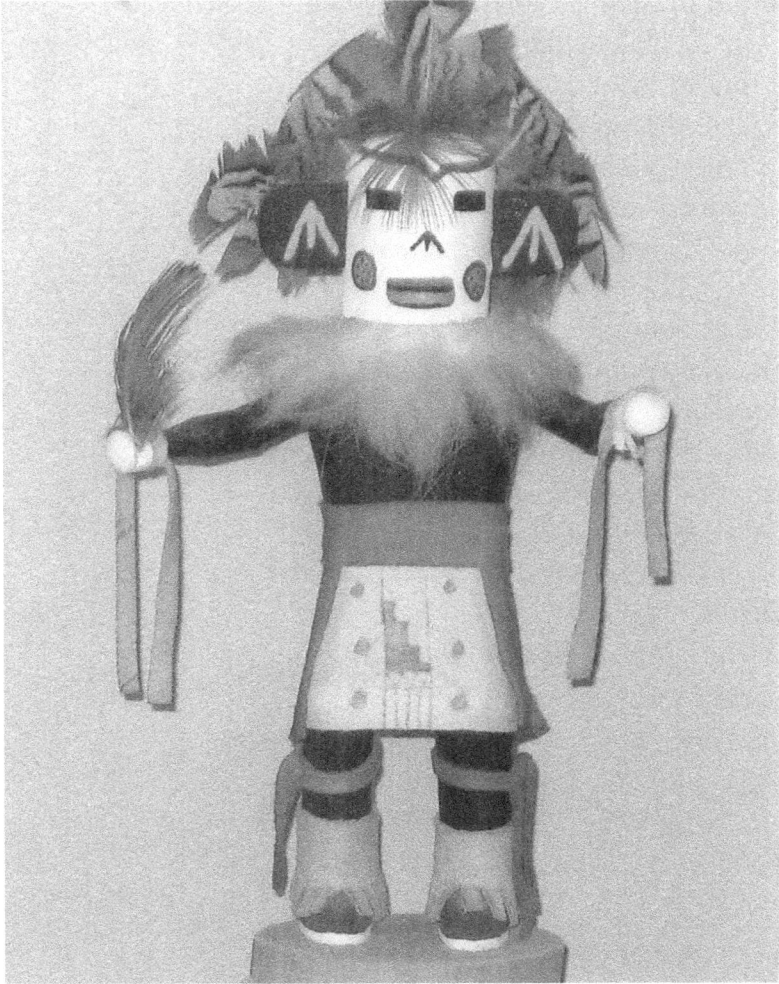

MY HOPI KACHINA, "ANGWUSH" (CROW)

Breath Sounds

The old Hopi man is dying.
A rainstick turns over gently, slowly.
Near to his weathered brown ears
a rattle is shaken and shaken.
His son begins to sing, the language
has no rhythms: his voice rises sharp
then recedes with a breathing out,
lower then fainter, like the wind.

The old man lies still, his eyes closed.
The old woman stands next to the bed.
She has on her best turquoise and velvet,
but covers this fancy dress with an old
brown wool shawl, frayed on one end.
This edge she holds close to her face.

The woman's dark eyes reflect
bright lights of the hospital ceiling.
She does not cry; there is no frown and
somehow you know there never has been.
She stands silent and steady,
soft as the old man's breathing.
No pain. You can always tell by the breath.

When the ceremony to Comfort the Spirit
has finished, the room is silent.
Into this space the old woman
sighs a sound like this:
Humm.

6

ROADRUNNER, LIZARD

Sunset Badger

Heart of the Mountain,
GREAT BASIN NATIONAL PARK

In high desert country the air is thin and everything is re-vealed. At this remote park in Nevada, 7,000 feet high, you can watch storms approach, see lightning up on Mori-ah Peak, and watch the evening sky change color for hours. When night finally arrives, the sky becomes a bowl and you are a spark of life inside of it, and every bit of the black above is speckled with light.

Rangers like to hike to special sunset places, making almost true the cliché, "they are paid in sunsets." So Kim and I set off with plenty of time to get to the rock-strewn hill beyond the pinyon-juniper forest and past the dry wash with day-old mountain lion tracks. On top, we look for just the right group of sun-warmed rocks to lean against and soothe our backs. While we eat our picnic supper of bean and salsa burritos (the fuel rangers live on in remote areas) we prepare ourselves for tonight's show.

We notice that the flat area of sand next to us is occupied. Our eyes widen. We barely breathe. We look at each other, asking with our eyes, "What do we do now? Is it alive?" For a long time we just look. Then we become braver (or impatient —are they sometimes the same?) and move closer to study the animal. It is a huge badger lying on its belly, limbs splayed out to the sides, eyes closed, its fearsome mouth opened a tiny bit. We whisper our observations, our questions, and our wonderment. The badger shows no sign of death, no injury. It looks comfortable and peaceful.

The badger is facing east. I think of Jake, an old Paiute Indian, who once said to me that when he goes to his death, he will climb a hill, face east, and lie down to die. Kim and I feel that we are in a church, or at a funeral of an important being, or in the veil between the worlds. We are enveloped by a rose and violet sunset. We don't need to say prayers tonight. We have entered grace.

Road Trip Stories

In an old car, you can drive cross-country, unhurried, in about five days. Longer, if the car breaks down. I drove back and forth across this country many times during my park service years. Sometimes I stayed out west for a year or two, but always returned home and worked here for a while. Each time I'd leave to go west, friends would come by to say goodbye and give me things that might be useful: a roll of duct tape, warm socks, sunscreen, stamps, a tiny stuffed bear and a squishy frog, and some healthy food for the road.

The car had to hold all my uniforms, backpacks, clothes, bedding and basic household items (rangers usually get minimally furnished housing, but you need to bring everything else with you); I even managed to fit in cross-country skis and snowshoes. You never know when a great opportunity might come your way and you don't want to miss it for lack of necessary equipment or clothes. When I finally left, the car was packed tightly, a cooler with five days of food sat on the

passenger seat, the car-top carrier was full, and my trusty bicycle was well secured on the back. One friend who came by to watch and help with the loading-up process wistfully said, "I'd give anything to do what you are doing: travel, and be a ranger at National Parks." My friend had a secure well-paying job with benefits. I said, "Well, drive an old car, live on minimum wage with no benefits or job security, and maybe you too could be a ranger." This truth hit home and we both laughed.

I was in my 40s when I began this uncertain, seasonal lifestyle. The unpredictability of weather, combined with driving an old car without AAA, a credit card or cell phone, made for some interesting times on the road and gave me an additional experience of this country and its people.

I always got a little nervous when I approached Kansas. More than once, in the spring, I drove across that state behind or in front of a tornado and once, in early spring, there was a tremendous blizzard, a complete white-out with extremely high wind. I thought about pulling off to stop in the breakdown lane, but just then police cars with flashing lights up ahead directed all the traffic to get off at the next exit. The road was closed beyond that point. It was in the middle of nowhere, but there was one small motel. I pulled into what might have been a driveway and stopped in an open area. When I tried to open the car door, I couldn't. The wind and snow was that intense. Within a few minutes, the trucker who had driven in behind me was opening the door. "Grab your stuff, come on, I'll help you."

My pack was always ready with basic necessities (you learn to be prepared as a ranger), and as I took his hand, he put his arm around me, almost lifting me out of the car while he held the door open. The wind, I'm sure, would have blown me over. Through the thick snow we noticed a line of five or six people forming a chain to grab us and then gradually pull us into the motel.

It was a very cold night. The motel owners brought out every available blanket and we all had a place to sleep, sharing rooms and space in the lobby. The next morning was clear. We were directed to a small breakfast place across the street where they offered hot drinks and free donuts before we all said goodbye and got back on the highway.

Camping was fairly easy to do in the fall, but early spring usually meant looking for a cheap motel. One very long driving day, on a two-lane road in Missouri, I could not locate a motel that was within my budget, so I pushed on, finally stopping, exhausted, at the only place I could find. It was cheap. But as I settled in, eating supper from supplies I had with me, there was a major ruckus in the next room. Soon there was yelling, cars peeling out, and what sounded like distant gunshots. I waited until things settled down, packed up, quietly went to my car in the dark, and drove off. I felt tired and stuck.

After 20 or 30 miles I spotted a little farm store and went in just as they were closing up. I asked if there were any inexpensive places to stay nearby. The woman said, "No, not for another 40 miles." I knew I couldn't keep driving and told her what had happened.

"Do you have a tent?" she asked. I told her I did and she showed me a place behind the barn, out of the wind, where I could set up for the night. "You'll be safe here, dear, we're just across the field." She pointed to a farmhouse nearby. It was cold, but with layers of clothes and my warm sleeping bag inside a bivey sack, I slept very well and woke to the most beautiful sunrise.

In Nebraska, on another small road (my preference whenever possible), I found "Bingo's". The old couple that owned this motel with only a few rooms had named it after their dog, and they were in business, not for money, but for the enjoyment of meeting people since they were no longer able to travel themselves. They wanted to know all about me, where I was from and where I was going, and when they learned I was a ranger, they had lots of questions. I explained that I was very tired and needed to take a little walk and get to bed early. "Come have a little breakfast with us in the morning and you can tell us more about your ranger life," the man said, and his wife nodded enthusiastically.

At 7a.m. in their sweet little house, I not only had the best meal of my five days on the road, but was also given a bag of food they had packed for me to take along. There were hugs when I left and I felt like I'd had a visit with family.

One spring, during the 2,800 mile drive to Nevada, I had been following, or chased by, tornadoes all across Kansas, and there was car trouble daily. When weather and finding a mechanic are top priority, there's not much time left to rest, eat, or walk and stretch.

Saturday afternoon, on what was to be my last long travel day, the car began to lose power on Highway 70. Luckily, it was right at an exit for Green River, Utah (next exit about 60 miles). The motor cut out as I coasted downhill toward town and the car came to a stop exactly in front of a large Truck Stop. There was a big rig pulling in, and I noticed a convenience store off to the side. I went in and asked if they worked on small cars too. "Nope," the woman replied." I sighed. "Is there another garage in town, then?" "Oh no, honey, you'll have to wait till Monday, they've already gone home. And tomorrow is Sunday, you know." I thanked her, walked back outside, and that's when the tears started.

An old man was sitting on a bench outside the small store, smoking a pipe. "What's the matter, little lady?" he asked. Perhaps it was the hunger and the exhaustion, coupled with feeling very alone that made his voice sound so very kind. I took a seat next to him and explained my dilemma through sobs: "My car's been breaking down almost every day, I'm running out of money, and I have to be at Great Basin

National Park to start my ranger job Monday morning."

"Are you hungry?" he asked. I nodded, "A little."

He patted my knee, "Wait here," then disappeared inside the store and returned with a grape ice pop and a package of peanut butter crackers for me.

"Now, let's see what we can do about your grumpy ole car." He walked over toward the big opening where trucks pull in for service, and by the time he returned, I had finished my snack, and looked up to see the big rig backing out. "Go on over there," he said, as I noticed two mechanics and the trucker pushing my car into the huge garage bay.

The mechanics worked on the car for over an hour, and then told me they didn't have the parts to repair the problem they had found in the cooling system, but they rigged something together for a temporary fix. "No charge." They told me I'd have to stay the night and get going about 3 a.m. to drive the six hours in cool air to the park, in Baker, Nevada.

I had only $30 in cash left, and not much in my checking account because of all the repairs along the way. I asked if there was a cheap motel. "Just a minute, mam." The two mechanics disappeared inside the office and came back with directions to a close-by motel. "Tell them you're the one sent by Dave and Zane. They've got a cheap room for you. Good folks there."

I thanked the men, told them they were my angels and said I'd like to send them a check for their work and time after I get paid in a few weeks. "No need," they smiled. "Good luck. You'll be all right if you can do your driving before the sun comes up too much."

I arrived okay, moved into ranger housing, started my job weary, but on time, and the car eventually got fixed. I made a thank you card for the mechanics and sent a large homemade healing salve. The package was addressed to:

Dave and Zane
Angels at Green River Truck Stop
Green River, Utah

In my travels I had met America and learned that most people are good and kind and honest. I sort of knew that already, but now I had a lot of personal experience to prove it.

Rattlesnake Rescue

I find a small snail on a dirt road and watch it for quite a while. Calming and centering, it becomes my meditation time today. The snail doesn't move from the road and it's too slippery to pick up gently, so I transport it using a leaf, walk it to the woods and leave it there to hide.

Creatures that are stressed will generally calm down when they are covered. That's why you'll see bird rehabilitators use a cloth to cover the rescued bird, no matter how large or small it may be. I once held a very stressed-out hummingbird that had flown into the visitor center and became trapped there, flying round and round, exhausting itself, as it tried to find a way out. When I finally captured it, I cupped both my hands around the bird to make a dark cave. Its little heart was quivering but the wings became still and when the bird seemed rested enough, I walked it outside to a trail and placed it on a shrub. It sat there a while before flying off. Visceral memories often remain strong; I can feel that oh-so-light tiny being in my hands as I write this.

At a park in high country, Nevada, backcountry ranger and firefighter Carrie and I often adventured together, on foot or on our bicycles. We had bonded the first week at the park after hiking in snow at 10,000 feet and losing our way as twilight crept upon us. We had no packs or flashlights because we had planned to do "just a little exploring." But this was extremely vast wilderness; lose your sense of where the only road is and you could be dangerously lost for a long time.

We kept our wits about us, both pretending bravery (as

we found out later) so as not to frighten the other about how dire our situation was. Each of us thought our fellow ranger was so smart and experienced that of course we'd be just fine. At one point my foot sank into heavy wet snow up to my knee, and I couldn't move because my foot had become pinned under a rock. Carrie, 25 years old, six feet tall, and very strong and capable, just wiggled me a bit and then lifted me straight up to where I was able to stand again. I said, "Let's follow that drainage (a small brook). It'll take us downhill to the road." I had no idea if it really would, but we got lucky and found the road just as darkness fully descended. From then on, we were ranger buddies all summer and managed to get the same days off so we could play and adventure together.

We frequently rode our mountain bikes through the 5,000-foot high desert, crisscrossing small dirt roads that ran past and through large ranches. Carrie would sporadically call out "Horny toad ahead!" (that's a horned-toed lizard), or "Rattler on the right!" Then we'd go into our rescue mode. These creatures lounging in a comfortable place would be squished if one of the large ranch trucks came along. Carrie's heart was far softer than her outward tough-as-nails attitude, and she knew exactly what to do, even with the rattlers: Take a stick, tap the ground behind the snake, while moving slowly closer to it and speak kindly, telling it to "move along now." And so, I learned.

We gradually became acquainted with many of the ranchers, most of whom were not crazy about the national park and all its restrictions, but they seemed to put us in another category. We made them laugh.

"Never know when I'm gonna run into you two!"

"Whadda ya doing way out here? Herding some more of our rattlers?"

They thought rescuing snakes was pretty funny. And we thoroughly enjoyed talking with those locals who knew this land well.

We also rescued rattlesnakes from the more heavily traveled trails up in the park when visitors reported them. Once a young boy and his little sister came running up to me, grabbing at my pants' legs, and close to tears, blurted out, "Ranger, come quick, they're scaring the snake real bad!" Sure enough, there was a small group of people surrounding a rattlesnake that was coiled and rattling.

"Don't let it get away, it's dangerous!" one man yelled to another who had picked up a stick. What did he think he was going to do? Bop the snake on the head?

Only the children seem to realize that the snake was more scared than the people were. Cornered and ready to strike, that was one stressed-out snake. When finally a park cop showed up to disperse what had become an over-curious crowd, the snake calmed down and glided to safety under a small sage bush. But it had to be moved to a backcountry area where it would not pose a danger to people, and where people would not be a danger to the snake.

The children, who were joined by a few more now, stayed to watch with great interest how rangers capture and transport rattlesnakes. We showed the kids the special stick with a loop on the end (like a little lasso) that we used to pick up the snake so we could put it into a soft but thick enough bag, and tie an overhand knot in the top so the snake would not slip through the opening. We explained that the snake would remain very still as it rode in a park truck over the bumpy road to a new home, far from trails and people, where it could live safely.

Gradually, I became more familiar with the local rattlesnakes, which were non-aggressive and generally shy, and I appreciated how they rattled a warning so you knew they were there. I wanted park visitors to also become more comfortable, so I started doing "Snake hikes" for visitors to

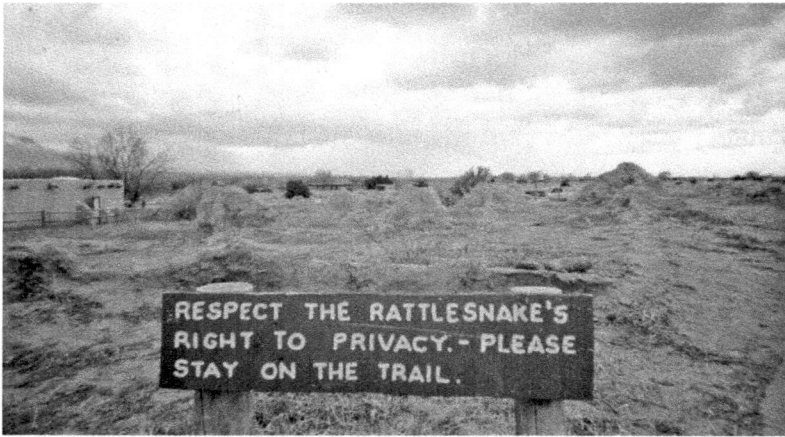

RESPECT THE RATTLESNAKE'S RIGHT TO PRIVACY. - PLEASE STAY ON THE TRAIL.

teach them how to move safely through rattlesnake country, by using a stick to tap in front of them while walking through tall grass and brush, or over large rocks and logs. I explained that the snake could only strike about half its length after it coiled, but it could strike in a flash.

"All you have to do is warn a snake that you're there, and the snake will leave. They know you aren't food, so as long as they don't feel threatened, they'll speedily depart. Rattlesnakes are really polite," I added. "They warn you by rattling if you get too close." I told them that it took me a while to become comfortable around rattlers and it helped me to remember what I once heard Old Pete from North Dakota say: "It just makes me happy clear through when I see one. They are such gentle animals. They do everything they can to avoid you."

At the end of the summer, while camping at a small, isolated state park I had an experience that let me know that I had finally gotten past any remaining fears. After setting up my tent at dusk, I took off my boots and headed up to a knoll, without a flashlight and wearing flip-flops, to watch the rising moon. On the way back down to my tent, picking my way through low sage bushes, I heard a rattle in front of me. I looked down and saw a medium-sized rattlesnake where I was about to take my next step. "Thank you for the warning," I said and walked about two feet to the right while the snake uncoiled and slowly moved two feet to the left and settled there.

"Goodnight, my friend," I said, and calmly continued on my way back to the tent.

A Story of Beavers

My old Navajo friend, Tucsohn, asked me to write to him when I went back to my home in the East. "My cousin will read it to me," he said. Since much of our time together was telling each other stories, he Navajo, and me Irish (he preferred hearing these in "the language of your people," a brogue), I decided my letter would be a story of a place where I often walked.

Beaver lived with his wife and uncle for many years by the side of the great pond. One day the people made a road not so far away.

When the children of the beaver were in their second year, they had to leave their home and make a new place for themselves. They chose a place between the large pond and the road. There they dammed the water with twigs and mud, and chewed down trees and branches to build a new lodge.

The people in the town were afraid this new little pond would grow larger and the water would come onto their road, and so they tried to trap the young beavers. But the beavers were sly; they swam around the traps or under them. The people-who-loved-the-road tried all through the spring and fall to catch the beavers, but they were not as smart as the water animals.

After the time of frozen ground, when the thunder came again, the road people hired a man who knew all about beavers and this time the young beavers were caught. They were taken to a pond far away, in a woods where there are no roads.

The older beavers did not like this and so two years later, after the birth of their new children, they told the young ones to make their home on the far side of the great pond, away from the road and the people. This they did.

Now the young beavers lived in new ponds that were far back in the woods, protected by a steep hill where it was difficult for the people to go. The road people had become weak because they did not walk; they traveled only in cars. They put away their traps because they thought the beaver problem was solved.

The traps grew rusty, the people drove their cars on the road, and the beavers lived in their hidden lodges.

Sometimes the-one-who-walks would go quietly through the woods and down the steep hill to sit and watch the beavers. She did not tell the people-who-loved-the-road that there were new faraway ponds with many beavers swimming in the waters.

Three Women

Smith Creek Canyon is not near anything, but anyone who lives in this wild place can tell you how to get there.

"Turn off at Highway 50 (aka "The loneliest highway in America"), take the cut-a-cross road, the one lined with tall sunflowers and red bee balm, and when you see the place where the kit foxes have denned up the past two years, turn onto the two-track road. That'll lead you through the desert, past Warm Springs (you can stop for a dip in the healing waters), past the Howell ranch, and just when Mount Moriah rises high and purple in front of you, look for the old wagon wheel that marks where the turn-off to the canyon is. There's barely a track there, but you'll see it, if you're looking for it. If you miss the turn-off, you'll soon get to the small tribe that moved away from the Shoshone Reservation and set up on this side of the mountain. Those folks will help you find your way back. They know that territory better than the lions that live up there."

JoAnne, Dorie and I borrow an old truck that wouldn't complain about a few more scratches and dents on its rusty metal and, with lots of food to share and enough water to last more than a day, we set off for our picnic, out there in the no-where. There are exactly 20 years between us, me in the middle.

JoAnne, in her 70s, has dark, muscled skin that is explained by her western hard-working life. Her mostly brown hair is in an off-centered ponytail; her eyes speak with tenderness and laugh more loudly than her quiet voice.

Dorie, in her 30s, is a park researcher who knows the

name of every rock, bird, plant and tree, and she carried most of our group supplies on her small, strong back. Her eyes are dark and shiny. "I'm the only Jew in Nevada," she says. "Me and the peregrine are being reintroduced."

DORIE AND JOANNE, AT DORIE'S HOUSE

We enter the trailhead to begin our adventure—a day to wander and explore the trees and plants in a pristine environment, and to search for the ancient cave paintings near the stream and the petroglyphs that we were told are high up the steep rocky slope on a cliff wall we will spot from below. As the day wears on, we grow tired and sore, but rest in the comfort of knowing that each of us would willingly care for the other with skill if any one of us got into trouble. That knowledge sets us free to laugh and sing and talk, and to tell our stories: stories of our generations, what delights us and what we are passionate about, and of how we each found our way and how we gathered strength to get there. To here, where now we three have bonded, in a far-off place that feels like home.

We walk slowly the last mile back to the truck. JoAnne leans against the door, I hand the packs to Dorie, and she throws them into the back of the truck and covers them with an old tarp that will keep the road dust from settling on our possessions. Dreamily, we three stand quiet, breathe the air, and let our eyes fall on this wild landscape all around us. We're tired, but we don't really want to leave just yet.

"What's that, up there?" Dorie is pointing to what looks like a cave.

"Think there may be some undiscovered rock art inside it, on the walls?" I ask.

"Could be something worth exploring, but I'm bushed," JoAnne says. "I'll wait here and guard the truck."

We three burst out laughing at the thought that this old clanky truck needs any protection way out here.

"Oh yeah, the antelope might want to take it for a joy ride and leave us stranded, far from the bus line," I tell my friends. And we can't stop laughing.

Eventually, we decide that since we're here, now is the time to check out the cave. Dorie and I start up the steep slope, sun heating up our backs. About half-way up, I call to Dorie, who has been ahead of me for a while, and signal for her to keep going, I'll wait right here.

She's like a mountain goat, climbing the steep hill with apparent ease. When she disappears inside the cave, I wave to JoAnne, who waves back with enthusiasm. Dorie reappears after several minutes and begins sliding downhill with side steps on the rocky scree. When she reaches me, I am handed a small pipe, it smells like sage and smoke and old wood, and then I show her the green heart-shaped rock that I found while waiting. She says there were only a few, mostly faded pictographs, but there was also an unusual petroglyph, very well preserved. She'll wait till we get down and tell us all about her findings.

Back at the truck, JoAnne has some cookies that she'd been saving for the long bumpy ride home to share with us. "Now, let's go home," she says and takes her seat behind the wheel. "Tell me everything you saw, on the way up, and what you discovered once you got there."

JoAnne has been thinking about what a beautiful metaphor for aging we three exhibited on this final exploration: her resting, me going only as far as I felt I could, and the youngest happily going on to explore and report back her discoveries.

JOANNE AND DORIE IN SMITH CREEK CANYON

Remember the Source
While Leaving Las Vegas

See this stone of bright blue with streaks of silver and white?
Notice when the water recedes from the shallow hole
it reveals itself to be plain grey rock.
Old as these hills.

Believe this desert land will remain even as the casino carves
another grand fountain and a greener golf course dotted with sand.
They are called sand pits, but the lizards know
this is home.

Remember how your feet were planted here even before
you came to understand the snake, the pronghorn, the dry heat.
Trust that your heart is big enough to imagine this land
back to its beginning.

Time Out

Day after day the great blue heron stands still
with feet in the mud at the edge of the bay.

A pelican swims in wide arcs, lifts off, spreading
its heavy wings, then quickly dives down, gulps a fish
and circles on the water's surface once again.

The heron has not moved.

An old bearded fisherman rows a small paint-chipped
skiff between white motorboats with names hopeful
of how-life-could-be, then continues meandering the
waterway, through yachts taller than the house he lives in.

Heron stands and watches.

At 7AM the sun lifts above the horizon and slides gold
into a ribbon-thin cloud opening in the grey
dome sky that covers all of Sarasota.
Cars speed by, unaware of beauty just beyond their metal.

Then, suddenly, the wind shifts and ushers in a change:
Cars in the road all stop at once. The people get out,
forgetting to close the doors. Leaf blowers
are silenced, hedge trimmers stop working
and beep beep beeping trucks turn off their motors.
The people have all walked to the edge of the water,

119

they feel a softness and they breathe lightly.
Jaws drop, eyes smile, children point in wonder.
It is quiet and still; only water and sky move.

When the sun tucks behind the lowering clouds,
the people return to their machines and forget this pause.
At night they will dream of what they have seen, and waking
from a peaceful sleep they will feel a yearning, a longing
for something, or someplace, they cannot name.
Meanwhile the heron stands.
He has seen it all come and go, the changes, the sameness.

And still, he does not move.

Rhythms

Now, you will go for a short walk, clouds form important shapes
requiring your attention, and when a bird calls and flies
into the woods, you will follow.

Trees will speak to you as old friends, earth will present
an abundance of lush green, all of which you will need to touch,
smell and look at for a very long time.

A poem begins in your head, where it simmers, unhurried,
until it has written itself. Now your steps have slowed, they are
as gentle on this earth as a soft spring rain.

Your eyes no longer look, now they receive.
The breath of a tiny breeze meets your skin and passes
through you. Long sighs are released in this quiet woods
and float away on leaves in the meandering stream.

Your body is light; your outer shell has melted and you
are no different from that oak, this moss, the bird,
and those clouds over your head.

No, it is not too much to ask:
To follow your rhythms and let life live you.

After Solstice

I turn too quickly:
life runs behind, unable to keep pace.
Sun, moon and stars hold the anchor firm
   and tether me to this place.

At the end of February, I will declare it spring.
Minutes hold full moments, the sun pauses
and the slumbering earth breathes deeply.
   We have come to rest here,
   now, in this light time.

Emerald Isles

Look now, as winter passes: green moss!
Here where the ice-melted brook
follows a winding downhill path
every pillow-shaped rock
capped with the promise of spring.
Smell: wet sponge, peat-thick, and alive!
Green-o-green. Oh!

Epilogue

When climbing mountains, it's good to know at what altitude you are likely to "hit your wall." That's when it becomes hard to keep going, through vertigo, nausea, and confusion, with feet that feel like lead. But often you do push on because you've learned how to and know that you can count on climbing companion(s), whose wall is beyond yours.

When backpacking, paddling, biking, or backcountry skiing, it's good to know where your edge is, when to stop and rest and how far you can push yourself, before total and unsafe exhaustion sets in. At 70 years old, I arrive at my wall much earlier and my edge has gotten closer, always within view now.

I am glad I adventured for years back then, and I tell younger friends, "Go now. Do your dream now, while you are in your 40s and 50s, your prime. It doesn't last forever, even though it feels like it will!"

What does remain, though, is the wonder and curiosity, continued learning, and new inner adventures. And yes, I still enjoy easy hiking, biking, skiing, paddling and being outside everyday to experience the natural world, which is as necessary to me as air.

Acknowledgements

When I tell Ellen and Susie that this book would not have happened without their very generous support and guidance, they don't believe me, but it's true!

Susie Patlove, poet, librarian and long-time friend, read every story and poem in this book, making comments, giving beautiful suggestions and encouragement. She gently pulled me along, telling me she wanted more pieces to read. When writing slowed for me, I felt an invisible hug and tug from Susie.

Ellen Eller has been the best editor I've ever had in the 30 years I've written for publications. She did the final reads, making corrections and giving suggestions for better clarity and flow. She's brilliant, an expert in all the little and big rules of writing. Did you know, for instance, numbers are spelled out up to ten, but higher than ten a numeral is used? Who could know such small, precise details? Ellen does. She is not only a professional editor, but also a friend who made it so interesting and fun. If there are any glaring mistakes on these pages, surely they are mine.

Several friends read stories early on and gave encouraging feedback. Thanks to Carol and Gregg and Will for informal and skillful reactions, Ned for his willingness and keen eye in finding those last few tiny errors (as well as his ongoing help with so many things for years).

I feel honored that my writer friends, and fellow meditators, Marian and Christian (see back cover) took an interest in my book; I've been a huge fan of their writing for years.

Maureen Moore, of Booksmyth Press, who lives up the road

from me, designed *What I've Seen* and was so good-hearted and patient with my minimal computer skills. Thanks, Mo.

My sister Mary and Richard gave me the use of their beautiful Florida condo for a week in February when it blew and iced and snowed back home. This book began in earnest there. And sister Pat always told me I'd write a book someday. She's my big sis, so I try to take her advice to heart.

There are so many friends, acquaintances, and strangers that over these many years have told me how they've enjoyed reading my nature columns. As any writer knows, it feels like a big hill of support under you when people read and enjoy your efforts.

My life has been enriched by all of the people here and out west that have befriended me (Margaret and all the folks in Baker, NV), and mentored me along the way. I've shared outdoor adventures with some brave and cheerful companions, too many to list, but ranger, naturalist and firefighter friends please know how much your companionship has nourished me all these years.

My family (oh, those little granddaughters!), and many cousins and friends have made my life full, as well as all of the Nolans who have followed their creative dreams. They have inspired and reminded me that we have that story-telling gene, whether for music or art or writing.

And finally, for those who are no longer here, my heart is grateful. Mom and Aunt Alice were unwavering in their understanding and interest in the path I took of least income in order to learn and experience what I love. Uncle Vinnie, my Dad's brother, had hoped I'd publish a book someday and sent a surprise check two weeks before he died. I am constantly amazed by my good fortune and unexpected blessings, and always by the natural world where I feel most at home.

ARCHES IPP   Colorado River

www.ingramcontent.com/pod-product-compliance
Lightning Source LLC
Chambersburg PA
CBHW022338280326
41934CB00006B/679